**ONCE
MORE
TO THE
RODEO**

WINNER OF THE PUSHCART PRESS EDITORS' BOOK AWARD

A MEMOIR

Calvin Hennick

ONCE MORE TO THE RODEO

PUSHCART PRESS   WAINSCOTT, NEW YORK

ISBN 978 1 888889 97 0

Cover and book designed by Mary Kornblum

Published by Pushcart Press
PO Box 380
Wainscott, NY 11975

Distributed by W.W. Norton & Company
500 Fifth Avenue
New York, NY 10110

Some names have been changed to protect the privacy of individuals.

For Nile.

Day 1

I CAN'T EVEN get us out the door right.

The road trip has been planned for months. Every night at bedtime, my five-year-old son Nile has told me how he's going to fall asleep and dream about all the fun we'll have on our way to Iowa, all the motel pools we'll swim in, all the treats we'll eat, all the games we'll play. But now that the rental car is parked in the driveway, I'm rummaging through drawers, randomly tossing socks and wrinkled tee shirts into my luggage, and I can hear Nile downstairs, pouting about how he doesn't want to leave his mother and little sister behind. It's late afternoon in late July, and sweat trickles down my back and pools in my boxer briefs as I struggle to zip up my suitcase. It's nearly four o'clock, and I want to get us on the road before the worst of Boston's evening rush hour hits.

"Ooooh," I hear Nile moan from his playroom. "It's just not fair."

"You're fine!" I call down to him, starting down the stairs with my bag. "We're going to have fun, remember?"

Nile answers in a low, despondent voice. "I just wish I could stay here with Mommy."

"Tough luck," I mutter to myself.

My expectations for this trip are impossibly high. We'll be on the road for ten days, headed toward the annual rodeo in my tiny hometown of Maxwell, Iowa. Nile starts kindergarten in a few weeks, and as absurd as it sounds to say out loud, I have the feeling that I'm sending him "out into the world" for the first time, that the protective bubble I've placed around him his entire life is beginning to pop. Nile is already becoming the man he's going to be, and while this is exciting to watch, it's also scary. As his father, I'm in charge of teaching him how to be a man, and although I think I'm doing okay so far, I'm also largely making things up as I go. The way I see it, I face three big obstacles. First, I have no relationship with my own father, and grew up with very little in the way of positive male role models. Second, I think that societal expectations of men are changing rapidly, in ways that we mostly aren't talking about yet. And third, Nile is a brown boy in a world where that still very much matters, and I have nothing to teach him about how to be a black man in America. For me, this trip is a quest, and although my goal feels unrealistic, it is also crystal clear. I want to figure out for myself what it means to be a good man right now, and what it means to raise one.

I load up the car in four or five sweaty trips, and eventually I'm as confident as I'll ever be that I have all my chargers, all my toiletries, all the snacks I've bought. If I've forgotten anything, I can pick it up on the road, and I know that Nile, at least, will have everything he needs. My wife, without being asked, packed his bag more than a week ago. Belzie kept her last name when we got married, and has often earned more money than me, and I'm an involved father who tries to do my share of the housework. And yet, we often find ourselves lapsing into familiar gender roles, almost unconsciously. Belzie is the one who packs the kids' bags and makes their lunches and picks out their clothes, and I'm the one who mows the lawn and manages our bank accounts and fixes things around the house (or, at least, I'm the one who tries; the bathroom vent fan, still not operational after months of my interventions, is a living testament to the limitations of my man-talents).

Belzie and our daughter are on the screened-in front porch when I come back inside, but Nile is still in the playroom, dolefully jabbering to himself. "Ready to go?" I call out.

"I go, too!" shouts my two-year-old daughter. Her name is Eloise, but we call her Peanut. Her brown curls are parted neatly down the middle and pulled back into two little afro poofs on the sides of her head, and her right arm is suspended in front of her chest by a navy blue sling, the result of a playground fall that fractured her clavicle two weeks ago.

"You and me will go out for Indian food," Belzie tells her.

"Want tikka masala," Peanut answers.

"Oooohh," Nile moans again. "I want chicken tikka masala, too."

The porch is stifling, and by now I'm sweating through my summer uniform of a gray tee shirt and cargo shorts, which I wear basically every day, even though I suspect that the outfit, combined with my burgeoning potbelly and poor posture, invites comparisons to Bobby from "King of the Hill." I have on an old pair of glasses, and I haven't touched my hair, which stands up on top of my head like a rooster's comb. Belzie, by contrast, looks as cool as always, lounging in a wicker chair in her sleeveless summer dress, her neat black braids hanging below her shoulders. Her skin is a dark brown. Both kids were born as pink and splotchy as me, but their complexions have since settled into a golden tan, and Nile seems to still be getting darker as he grows up.

"Got everything?" Belzie asks me, nodding to the car parked in the driveway.

"Probably not."

"Your phone charger?"

I nod.

"Did you get the sunscreen?"

"Yes."

"Are you sure?"

"I have the sunscreen."

"Make sure to use it."

Unlike me, Belzie is pensive and quiet, and as always, most of what she means in this interaction is left unsaid. And what's left unsaid is this: As much as we love each other, we both love our children more; and that as much as I love them, Belzie loves them more than I do; and that it's nice that I want to take this father-son road trip with Nile, but that I'm not doing it the way she would do it, which is to plan every hotel, every restaurant, every gas stop in advance; and that that's basically okay, but that if I drive her firstborn child halfway across the country without even inviting her to come along, then I'd damn well better return him without so much as a scrape or a sunburn.

I poke her shoulder and smile. "Hey, I'm not the one who was with Peanut when she broke her clavicle."

The sounds of Nile muttering to himself waft in from the playroom. I can't quite make out the words, but it sounds almost as though he's saying individual, mournful goodbyes to each of his toy police cars and camper vans and front loaders. He's a sensitive, big-hearted kid, quick to fall in love with new people and places, and, much like his father, he lacks a talent for gracefully handling disappointment. He hasn't yet figured out – or, at least, hasn't learned to accept – that disappointment is inevitable, that even if he gets everything he wants most in life, he will still have to give up other things he wants just a little less. He doesn't understand why everything can't be absolutely perfect.

Sometimes, I worry that this guileless tenderness of his will get him eaten alive when he goes out into the world, but at the same time, a part of me worries that he'll lose it. He's slowly getting better at managing his emotions, and it's actually a little bittersweet for me to see. He had a long, tumultuous toddlerhood, and when he threw tantrums, I would have to pin his arms and legs and fold his body and carry him in front of my chest to keep him from hurting himself or me, sometimes walking home a quarter mile from the playground like this, cursing under my breath while he bucked and screamed, trying to get free. During one four-month period, he woke at 4:30 every morning and shrieked as loudly as he could for an hour or more, for no reason that I can remember now.

There's a scene in the second "Kill Bill" movie where Uma Thurman and a one-eyed Daryl Hannah battle to the death in a trailer containing a loose black mamba, and Thurman snatches Hannah's remaining eyeball out of her head, and then Hannah goes completely batshit crazy, shrieking and thrashing and kicking and flailing, trying in her blind, hysterical rage to inflict as much damage as possible onto the rest of the world before she dies. That's exactly how Nile acted every time we made him quit playing and go to the bathroom when he was three years old.

Don't get me wrong. I'm glad those days are over. Entire months passed when I wasn't able to enjoy him at all – this person who I loved more than anything, even when he was swatting my glasses off my face and kicking me in the groin – and twice, when I was completely out of ideas, I broke my no-spanking rule (which, in addition to making me feel like a terrible father, elicited outraged cries from Nile. *You broke my butt! Daddy, don't hit me! Daddy, don't break my butt!!!*) Still, there's something sad about Nile learning to tame himself, learning to act as though his feelings don't matter.

I go to Nile in the playroom and squat down so I can look him in his eyes, which are squinty like my own but brown like my wife's, and I run a hand through his short black curls. He's wearing cutoff shorts and a striped tank top. I rest my other hand on his bare, bronzed shoulder, darker than usual from the summer sun. Sometimes this gentle touch is all he needs to recenter himself. When he was a toddler, I would sometimes lie down right on top of him, propping myself up a bit on my elbows, but resting a good deal of my heft on his little body, like a weighted blanked, and it would help him calm down. Belzie and I tried timeouts for a while, but they amped Nile up rather than settling him. Often, I'll just call him over to me and give him a big bear hug when he's having a rough day. I lift him up, and he wraps his legs around my waist and buries his face into my neck, and I squeeze him as tightly as I can without crushing his little ribs.

I worry that I'm coddling him. But he's five years old. Maybe he needs me to coddle him.

"Hey, buddy," I say.

"Hi, Daddy," Nile says, his voice as vulnerable as a wounded deer. "Do you want to see my Lego city?"

He's stalling me. It's already a couple of minutes past four o'clock, and we should be on the road. But I indulge him for a minute. His creations are legitimately impressive, much more intricate than anything I can put together without instructions. It's a little weird that he's already surpassed me at something, even if it's only Legos. "Sure, baby," I say. "Show me what you've got."

Every last inch of the white Ikea bookshelf is covered in the colorful bricks. "This is the people on the moving walkway in the airport," Nile says. "And this is the ladder truck, rushing off to the emergency. And this is the police chief car, coming to the rescue."

"All right, baby," I say. "Now it's time to go put our shoes on."

"And this is the moon buggy."

"Nile."

"And this is the tow truck, towing the convertible."

"Nile." I put my hand on top of his head again. "It's time to go."

"Oh," he whimpers. "But I want to go to the restaurant go with Mommy and Peanut."

"Listen," I say. "I want to tell you a secret."

Nile looks up at me. "What is it?"

I crouch down again to meet his eyes. "In the whole history of the world, did you know that nobody's ever had more fun than we're going to have on this trip? This is going to be the most fun anybody's ever had. Ever."

I'm mostly honest with Nile, but at times I turn into a one-man propaganda machine. Whenever I eat broccoli or cauliflower, I draw attention to it, saying, "Daddy loves vegetables!" (I want to be a good role model, or, failing that, pretend to be one.) And then the next day, I'll ask him, "What's Daddy's favorite food?" and he'll shout, "Vegetables!" all enthusiastically, even though he can plainly see me shoving pizza and ice cream into my face. He believes me more than he believes his own eyes. And so I decide that this is how he will remember this trip. It will be the most fun anybody's ever had.

"Will it be more fun than a shuttle bus ride to the airport?" Nile asks me.

"Even more fun than that," I say.

"Even more fun than riding a city bus?"

"If you can believe it." I take his hand. "Come on, let's go put on our shoes."

"Okay." Nile squeezes my hand and begins walking with me to the door.

"Hey buddy," I say. "Who has more fun than us?"

Nile looks up at me, his eyes still a little moist. "No one, Daddy."

• • •

In his essay "Once More to the Lake," E.B. White laments the fact that his son has "never had any fresh water up his nose," and takes him to a lake where White's family vacationed when he was a boy. During the week they spend at the lake, White watches in astonishment as his son seems to transform before his eyes into White's childhood self. I don't expect (or even particularly want) Nile to "become" me on this trip, but I share White's impulse to take my son on a pilgrimage back to a place that was significant to me when I was a boy, and to see whether the trip has anything to teach me. Nile's upbringing, so far, is totally different from my own. I grew up in a town of 800 people in the Midwest, and he's an East Coast city boy. My parents were divorced and white; Belzie and I are married, and she's from Haiti. My parents held a series of working-class jobs; Belzie is a teacher, and I'm a freelance writer who quit covering suburban news for the Boston Globe and started writing tech content for corporations after I acquired a family and a mortgage. When I was a boy, I had free run of the neighborhood, wandering in and out of yards and playing war and hide-and-seek with other kids, whereas Nile is supervised every moment of his life.

If E.B. White wanted to see what happened when his son got some fresh water up his nose, I'm curious to see how Nile handles his first whiff of pig shit.

We make our way out of town in the rental car, a black Toyota Avalon with twelve thousand miles on it, heading for I-95 on our way to Route 20. I haven't planned out any real path, but I'd like to stick mostly to smaller, scenic roads, keeping away from the interstate as much as possible. Route 20 is a historic coast-to-coast highway, and it will take us all the way to Iowa if we let it.

"Can I have some chocolate milk?" Nile asks from his booster seat in the back.

"Sure, baby." I reach over and flip up the top of the red Coleman cooler, which I've loaded with ice, boxes of chocolate milk, cans of seltzer water, and, in a moment of ridiculous optimism regarding the likely healthfulness of the food choices I'll make over the next ten days, some carrots and hummus. On the floor of the back seat sits a brown paper bag bursting with Goldfish crackers and granola bars and single-serving bags of pretzels, alongside a plastic Avengers shopping bag filled with sunscreen and bug spray and first-aid supplies. Our luggage – a big black suitcase for me and a smaller orange bag for Nile – is in the trunk, along with my shoulder satchel and a backpack. On the passenger seat next to me is a Michelin road atlas and two audio books that I've picked up for Nile – "Stuart Little" and "The Mouse and the Motorcycle" – which I'm pretty sure I thought were the same book until the moment I saw them sitting side-by-side at the library. Only now, glancing at the cover, do I remember the author of "Stuart Little." It was written by E.B. White.

My hand grabs hold of a chocolate milk in the cooler. I press the box into the steering wheel to stab in the straw, then pass the drink back to Nile. "Here you go."

Nile takes a sip. "It's cold."

"Too cold?"

"No." He takes another sip. "Not too cold."

I tell him not to spill in the rental car, or else we'll have to pay to have it cleaned, and he agrees to be careful.

"This car is just a little bit different from our other car," Nile says.

"From the Camry, you mean? They're both made by the same company."

"Yeah," Nile says. "It's just a little bit different from

the Camry. One thing that's different is that the green light doesn't come on when the car is driving."

"Oh." I have absolutely no idea what green light he's talking about. "Sure."

"The other thing that's different," Nile says, "is that the turn signal makes a different sound."

"Okay."

"And also, a thing that's different is that the speakers are in a different place than in the Camry car."

"That's enough things that are different." I flick on my turn signal and merge onto 95. We've lucked out. The southbound lanes are gridlocked, but our section is open road. "Why don't we come up with a nickname for the car? Do you want to help me come up with a nickname?"

Nile thinks for a moment. "Let's call it the Black Racer."

"The Black Racer," I repeat. "Does that mean it goes super fast?"

"Yeah, it goes super fast." He's quiet for a moment, and when he speaks again, his voice has turned sorrowful once more. "I wish I could be with Mommy and Peanut."

"Do you know what homesickness is?"

Nile says he doesn't, and I explain the concept to him, telling him that it's okay to feel a little homesick, but that he shouldn't let it ruin the fun of the trip. Trying to get him excited again, I go through our itinerary, telling him how we're going to spend a few nights on the road, stopping whenever we feel like it, and then meet up with Belzie and Peanut in Chicago, where they're flying to visit friends of ours who just had a baby. From there, Nile and I will drive on to Waterloo to see family, and then finally we'll arrive at my hometown of Maxwell, just in time for Old Settlers, an annual carnival with rides and games and a two-night rodeo.

"Oh," Nile says. "Are there any city buses?"

"Where?"

"In Iowa."

"I don't know if we'll see any city buses," I tell him. "Daddy grew up in a really small town. There aren't any city buses there. They have school buses. And tractors. Do you want to see a tractor?"

"Well, city buses are good," Nile says. "They help you move in cities, just like a taxi cab, or just like a subway. Sometimes they help you move to train station, and sometimes they help you move to airports."

Nile has been obsessed with transportation since he was old enough to be obsessed with anything. If I didn't know better, I'd assume that someone was pushing it on him, trying to make him as "boy" as possible, but this is just the way he is. His first words were *mama* and *dada*, but the first one he said consistently, and with enthusiasm, was *car*. He couldn't pronounce the "r," and so he sounded like a demented seagull, toddling around the neighborhood with Belzie and me, stopping at every vehicle, pointing and screeching, "CAH! CAH! CAH!"

"Maybe we'll see some of that stuff on the way," I allow. "But that's not what the trip is about. When we get to Maxwell, we're going to the carnival with the rodeo. Remember?"

"I remember," Nile says. "Do they have a Ferris wheel at the carnival?"

"I don't know," I admit. "They have rides, but I don't know if they have a Ferris wheel."

I haven't been back to Old Settlers in sixteen years, since the summer after I graduated high school, but friends tell me that it's gotten a little smaller each year. At its height, it was a legitimately impressive, even preposterous, celebration for such a small town, featuring not just the rides and games and the rodeo, but also hypnotists, and spelling bees, and tractor pulls, and talent shows, and stand-up comedians, and arm wrestling tournaments, and fireworks, and classic car shows, and even something called "Cow Chip Bingo," where otherwise sober and reasonable adults stood around a painted grid and placed bets on where, exactly, a well-fed heifer would take an enormous dump.

"The big thing is the rodeo," I tell Nile. "Do you remember what a rodeo is?"

"What is it?"

"It's a place where you go to watch people ride on horses." I realize that this may strike Nile as less-than-thrilling, and I try again. "You buy a ticket, and you watch people ride on horses. And bulls. People ride on horses and bulls."

"Oh."

I flail, trying to come up with a better explanation. It's been twenty years since I've gone to a rodeo, and I suddenly realize that I don't really understand the point. "Do you know what they used to do at the rodeo when Daddy was a little boy? They took a calf – that's a baby cow – and they covered it with strips of duct tape. And then all the children had to chase the baby cow around the rodeo and try to take off the tape while the cow ran away."

"Why?" Nile asks. "Did you do something wrong?"

"No, no, it was a game." Hearing the words come out of my mouth, it sounds absurd, like I'm making things up, or I'm an old man describing how things were in the 1940s. "If you pulled off a piece of tape, the guy from the rodeo gave you a two-dollar bill, and then you could use the money to buy a treat. If they still do the game with the baby cow, do you want to play? Do you want to win some money for a treat?"

Nile thinks. "I don't want to hurt the cow," he says, finally. "But I do want to play the game."

I smile, imagining Nile in a cowboy hat, chasing a calf around the arena. The rodeo feels like a fitting finish line for our trip, if only because the cowboy is the closest thing to a Platonic ideal of American masculinity. I doubt that we'll come home wearing chaps and spurs, but I have this crazy idea that I'll be watching some hapless cowboy sailing through the air after being bucked from his horse, and suddenly I'll grasp something I couldn't understand before. It's silly, this idea that there are some sort of Cosmic Answers about Manhood waiting in Iowa for us. I'm not even sure there are any answers. But maybe it's enough to spend this time with my son, thinking about the questions.

. . .

The interchange with Route 20 is a total nightmare of a braided offramp, with hundreds of cars all trying to switch between the two crowded lanes before they run out of runway. I finally white-knuckle my way into the exit lane, and I'm about to let out my breath as an SUV passes me on the right. The vehicle slides into the little pocket of space in front of me, and then immediately slams on its brakes. I nearly hit the person, and I slam on my own breaks, and the next car almost hits us, and then we're all at a standstill. I swear, it doesn't even seem like people are trying to get where they're going half the time. It's like they're just trying to cause accidents. That's one of the things I miss about Iowa, how it feels like there's enough room for everybody.

Eventually, we creep along again, but it turns out that this stretch of historic Route 20 is just a bunch of people trying to get back to their homes in the posh "W" suburbs at the end of their workweeks. We're not seeing America. We're seeing Jaguar and Bentley dealerships. Our average speed hovers around twenty miles per hour.

The SUV brakes suddenly again, and I give the steering wheel a light bang with my palm. "Maybe Route 20 wasn't such a great idea," I say to myself.

"Yeah," Nile answers from the backseat, overhearing me. "I don't see the ocean."

"No, the ocean is thousands of miles away," I tell him. "We're not going to see the ocean."

"If we cross a bridge over the ocean," Nile offers, "we could see an octopus."

The traffic picks up again, and I tentatively press down on the gas. "Probably not."

"Oh. Maybe we could see the fish."

"This road goes all the way across the country, but Iowa is in the middle of the country. No ocean."

"Are we almost in Iowa?" Nile asks.

"No, I told you. We have to go to Chicago first." I try to meet his eyes in the rearview, careful not to take my attention off the road for too long. "Remember, we're going to see Mommy and Peanut in Chicago?"

"Oh." Nile waits for thirty seconds, and then asks, "So are we pretty close to Iowa?"

"Can you please stop asking me that?"

"I WAS JUST ASKING!!!"

"If this trip is making you grumpy," I say, "we can just go home."

"I'm not grumpy," Nile says, his voice suddenly chipper again. "Oh look, I can see the ocean! See the blue stuff? "

"It looks blue in the distance, but that's a hilltop covered with trees."

"No, the BLUE stuff," Nile clarifies, as though I'm an idiot. "It's the ocean."

"Fine, fine," I say. "It's the ocean."

"I guess we must be getting pretty close to Iowa, then."

Eventually, Route 20 morphs from a bucolic commuter road into a sort of strip mall hell, crammed full of nail salons and Dunkin Donuts franchises. With the traffic, we haven't traveled very far, but it's approaching Nile's dinner time, and I begin to hunt for a place to eat. He's been begging for Indian food, but I don't want to have to hunt for a restaurant, and I talk him into McDonald's instead, promising him a strawberry milkshake for dessert.

The next set of Golden Arches is only half a mile up the road, and I pull off into the strip mall parking lot, where the McDonald's sits on its own little island. I park the Black Racer near the main strip mall and turn off the engine, and after all of these negotiations, I look up and see that – *of course* – I've parked directly in front of a restaurant called Tandoori Grill Indian Cuisine. "Change of plans!" I announce. "We're having chicken tikka masala after all."

The place is empty and dimly lit, and it's scandalously expensive for a dinner buffet in the suburbs. Briefly, I consider walking out and seeing what the Japanese place next door has to offer, but we're already here, and Nile wants Indian food, and he knows that his mother and his sister are back in Boston eating chicken tikka masala without him. I load up a couple of plates at the buffet and set up us in a booth against the wall. The sauces are bland and watery, and the pakoras are doughy and crunchless, but Nile doesn't seem to notice. I open up the road atlas on the table and begin to show him how far we've traveled (only a couple of inches on the Massachusetts map), and a woman who seems to be the restaurant owner comes over and sets a small Styrofoam coffee cup in front of him.

"Mango lassi," she announces.

Nile looks up at the woman, his face blank.

She beams at him. "It's like a milkshake!"

Nile sips the tiniest taste and puts a polite little look on his face and thanks the woman, and she leaves our table.

"You don't like it?" I ask him.

"I sort of like it," he says.

He obviously doesn't like it.

"It's like a milkshake," I say, parroting the owner. "You wanted a milkshake."

"It's not really like a milkshake." Nile pushes the cup away from him a few inches. "It doesn't really taste like strawberries."

I sigh and grab the cup from him and take a sip, not wanting the mango lassi to go to waste. The drink lights up my taste buds, and immediately I go back for more. It's the first sugar I've had in over two weeks. I'm constantly trying out some new "lifestyle change" (which usually really means "crash diet"), trying to get myself healthy and keep off the thirty pounds that I've lost and regained over and over again since college. At various times, I've gone vegan, done a sort of modified Paleo diet, and even, for a time, enthusiastically followed a plan peddled by a beady-eyed charlatan of a doctor who once tried to heal his own foot injury with a 46-day starvation and now sells his own line of salad dressings. Going sugarless is my latest attempt to manage this portion of my life, but as I drink down the mango lassi, I can feel my sense of control slipping away, and I know that I'll likely have to start all over again at the end of the trip.

Sugar is one thing. Alcohol is another. Since college, I've had trouble controlling my drinking, and the only thing I've found that works for me is to quit completely. Right now, I've been sober for three months, and I haven't been experiencing any real cravings. But I've been sober for much longer stretches than this in the past, and I know from experience that it's always easy, right up until the moment when it's not. When I'm drinking, I'll put down a whole pint of Jim Beam sitting by myself on the couch on a Tuesday night, looking through old photos or watching reruns of "Cheers" and "Roseanne," lingering in the warm, loose, nostalgic feeling that booze brings on for me. I'll have a beer with lunch, and then another, and then switch to whiskey, wasting an entire day. So far, the worst consequences of my drinking have been some nasty hangovers and speculative worries about my longterm health. I don't drive drunk, or get into bar fights, or cheat on my wife. I just drink. But I drink a lot, and once I start, I can't stop.

When I drink, I usually wait until the kids are in bed. Belzie doesn't say much when I come back from the liquor store with a six-pack of tallboys or a pint of bourbon, but I can see the worry in her eyes. I worry, too, about what will happen if I keep it up. I don't allow myself to think of the worst things. Getting divorced. Losing my family. Dying alone. But even without any of that, the thought of Nile and Peanut growing up and watching me drink myself into a stupor each night is enough to make me want to stop.

There are moments when I miss the booze a little, moments when I'm stressed out or tired and just want to turn off my brain and relax. But I'm confident I won't end up nursing a bottle of bourbon in a motel room on this trip while Nile watches cartoons. Right now, it feels like this will be the time I quit for good. But then, it always feels like that until it doesn't.

I'm constantly fighting battles in the war between the things I want to do and the man I want to be.

• • •

"Daddy?" Nile says between bites of tandoori chicken. "Will I be able to stay at my school for a long time?"

He means the preschool he's attended for the past three years. All his friends are there, and he loves the teachers, and although he claims to be excited to start kindergarten, he seems pretty anxious about leaving his old school behind. I'm a little anxious about it myself. His days at preschool are filled with play and fun, and in his entire time there, I don't know if a single person has ever been unkind to him. When I drop him off each morning, I have 100 percent confidence he'll be totally, totally fine. But everything ahead of us is unknown.

I hesitate with my answer. He only has three weeks left of preschool. "Sure," I say. "You'll stay there until September."

"That's a long time," Nile says, his voice matter-of-fact. "And that's good. Because I love my friends."

"Is your new school going to be scary?" I ask him. "Or is it going to be fun?"

I do this sometimes, give him little one-question pop quizzes with only one possible answer, trying to get him to see things my way.

"Fun," Nile says. "But I'm nervous. I don't really know how loud it's going to be in the cafeteria. Or how long is the circle time. Or how long is the lunch time."

"How long is the circle time?" I repeat, trying to make sense of his worries.

"And what if the cafeteria is so loud?!" Nile says.

"Why would the cafeteria be loud?" I ask him. "What makes you think that?"

"Because when I watched the 'Welcome to Kindergarten' video," he explains, "I figured out that the cafeteria is so loud!"

He's talking about a welcome video made by the school district. When Nile first watched it, he asked why the school was "so light," and it took Belzie and me a while to figure out that he was talking about how nearly all the children in the video were white. His preschool is like a little United Nations, and while our town is diverse, too, the diversity isn't distributed evenly. There are only four elementary schools in town. One of them is only 3 percent black, and another is 41 percent black.

When the time came to buy a house, Belzie and I considered staying in Boston, where she teaches middle school, but the district was between superintendents, and hadn't yet finalized its new school assignment and bussing plan. There were too many unknowns. The suburb where we live borders the city, and the diversity of the community was important to us when we were house-hunting, but it's been disappointing to see how people still find ways to sort themselves out by color, even in a smallish town with lots of families that look like ours. Occasionally, I play pickup basketball at the courts near the high school, just up the hill from our house, and nearly all of the kids who play are black. When I walk by Little League baseball games, nearly all the children are white.

Belzie and I found out a few weeks ago that Nile will be attending the "black" elementary school. Our house is in between two zones, and Belzie was hoping that he'd end up at the other possibility, which has less diversity than the school he'll attend, but higher test scores. All the people I've talked to – black parents, white parents, mixed families – say they love Nile's future school, and I was fine with the placement. Still, I was unnerved to find a news article from a decade ago, when some white parents in town threatened lawsuits and put their kids in private school to prevent them from being sent to the "inferior" school where my brown son will start in a few weeks.

I don't yet know the extent to which race will shape Nile's

experience of the world. We're taking this trip in the middle of the Black Lives Matter movement, and while there are entire books to be written about every case that has made national headlines these past few years – Trayvon Martin, Eric Garner, John Crawford, Mike Brown, Philando Castile, and far too many others – what I will remember most vividly about this period is how all of these young black men were labeled "thugs" after they'd been shot down in the streets by people who feared them. I watch Nile grow taller, and I see his skin grow darker, and I hold my breath.

"The cafeteria won't be scary, baby," I tell Nile.

"And I don't know how long lunch will take."

"Just eat, buddy." I feel like I shouldn't have started him talking about this. "Eat your food."

"And I don't know how long circle time will be!"

"Why are you worried about how long circle time will be?"

"Because I don't know how long it will be!" Nile says, throwing his hands up in the air. "Maybe too long? Maybe four more minutes?"

"It'll be fine." I don't know, of course, how long circle time will be. Or if this new school will actually *have* circle time. Or really, now that I think about it, what circle time even *is*.

I pass Nile a spongey pakora. "Just eat. Eat this. Here, here, eat this."

• • •

When Nile was born, I imagined him growing up to be a confident, self-assured kid, fortified by the constant affirmation of his two loving parents. But in reality, he's just as neurotic and anxious as I was at his age. Despite having a father around, he's an uncoordinated and indifferent athlete, and even though he's been in preschool for more than half his life, he lacks some basic social awareness. At the playground, he'll claim a group of skeptical seven-year-old girls as his "new best friends," or try to get the other boys to hold his hand. I wonder how long the other kids will tolerate his little weirdnesses.

In my own memory, the kids didn't get mean until around the third grade, but then they turned Lord-of-the-Flies vicious, seemingly overnight, as though some primal switch had been flipped in their brains. Third grade was the year that my mom packed my two younger brothers (they're twins) and me into the car and drove us away from Iowa. She and my father had divorced before I turned four years old, but had lived together on and off for the next few years, partly because it was easier to pay bills with two incomes, and partly because my mom wanted her boys to have a dad. But in the previous few months, his behavior had turned violent and scary, and my mom felt that the only way to protect herself from him was to get as far away as possible.

We landed in Rockport, Massachusetts, where my mom grew up. Rockport is a quirky little town on the tip of Cape Ann, part artist colony, part coastal tourist trap, part blue-collar fishing village. Its chief claim to fame is a little buoy-adorned red shack on the harbor called "Motif Number 1," which locals say is the "most-painted building in the world" (an assertion that struck me even in childhood as both unverifiable and wildly improbable). We lived with my Aunt Rhonda for a couple of months before moving into low-income housing, and it didn't take the other kids long to figure out that I was a fatherless, poor outsider. The other kids all paid for their lunches with crumpled, highlighter-covered dollar bills, while I paid with the blue plastic tokens that the school gave to the free-lunch kids. Somehow, the other children associated Iowa with pigs (Did a teacher tell them? Did they ask about Iowa, and a teacher said, *Oh, there's lots of pigs there?*), and they followed me around the hallways and the playground, pulling their noses up into snouts with their thumbs and oinking at me.

I didn't make things any easier on myself. I was a bossy, fussy perfectionist who never missed a chance to point out when someone else was wrong. I wrote poems about the fall leaves and insisted on reading them in front of the whole class, and I had weird little hobbies like growing my own crystals by dissolving sugar and salt in cups of water. At home, I was obsessed with getting enough sleep. I would put myself to bed at seven o'clock and then toss and turn for hours. If my younger brothers made any noise, I would stand at the top of the stairs and shout, "BE QUIET! I'M TRYING TO SLEEP!!!"

Each summer, my brothers and I spent weeks in Iowa with Papa and Alice. Papa was my father's father, and Alice was his second wife, married to him since before I was born. The summer days were long and idyllic. My brothers and I sprayed each other with squirt guns during the hot, humid afternoons, and then trapped fireflies in jelly jars at dusk. Near the end of the summer before fifth grade, I got the idea that I would be happier if I stayed in Maxwell with Papa and Alice instead of flying back to Rockport. My mom initially said no, but then, when school started and I was just as friendless and miserable as always, she relented. And so, in early October, I boarded a plane by myself, tagged along with a bored Delta employee during a layover in Chicago, and then arrived in Des Moines, where Alice picked me up from the airport and drove me home to Maxwell.

My mom still feels guilty about this, but I don't blame her for letting me leave. She can't stand to see any of her children unhappy. Today, my brothers and my mother and I all live in Eastern Massachusetts, and although I didn't live with the rest of them when I was a teenager, we're all fairly close, even if my relationship with my mom is perhaps less formal than most people's. This past Mother's Day, I bought her flowers, but forgot to grab a card, and she made a jokey little remark about how her *other* two sons had remembered. Sure, I said, but she didn't give them up for adoption. We laughed.

On my first day back in Maxwell, the other boys seemed excited that I'd returned, and they all talked about how we'd play football together at recess. But I'd never played football before. I'd never even *watched* football before. I didn't know the rules, and I quit after ten minutes, complaining that the game was "too confusing." That was it for me. I was doomed. I was the boy who thought football was too confusing.

I know I can't protect Nile from every little bit of adversity in life, and I know I shouldn't try. Part of growing up is learning to handle your own shit, and I'll have to find a way to let Nile learn to handle his. But I never want him to feel unsafe in the way that I felt during middle school, knowing that anybody could mess with me whenever they wanted. One day in the lunch line, two boys each took one of my arms and pulled them across my body, yanking as hard as they could for a full minute or more, until it felt like my shoulders would separate and my ribs would cave in. During a unit on the Holocaust, the other boys decided that I was "Jewish," and our gym teacher, a middle-aged former jock who was unnaturally obsessed with forcing us to shower after class, joined the kids in making fun of me, calling me "Rabbi Calvin Hennickstein" and "The Messiah." In guidance class one day, our teacher showed us an episode of "Degrassi Junior High" in the darkened band room, and the principal's son spent the entire period sneaking up behind my chair every few seconds, flicking at my earlobes and karate chopping my neck with both hands, until it felt like my entire head was on fire. I tried not to let the other boy see that I was crying, but the tears came faster than I could wipe them away.

I believe these memories are unremarkable, but that's only because all these things happened when I was a child. Imagine me going through my life now, having to deal with people putting duct tape in my hair at the grocery store, or shoving me into walls at the DMV, or teaming up and throwing their combined weight into me as the city bus rounded corners, so that my head slammed into the window and the air left my lungs. It would be madness.

Why do we take for granted that kids have to be so miserable?

• • •

Nile, nearly done with his food, has turned fidgety, and I keep having to tell him to get back in the booth. And then to stop lying down in the booth. And then to stop kneeling and smooshing his face down into the booth. He gets like this when he's tired, and he's probably acting out his homesickness a little bit. But that doesn't mean it's not annoying.

"Come here," I tell him.

Nile twists in his seat. "I don't want to."

"Come here."

Reluctantly, Nile comes over and sidles up next to me. I loop my arm around his back and hold him by his shoulder. "Listen to me," I say. "If you can't act right in restaurants, then we'll get food at the grocery store and eat in motel rooms. Is that what you want?"

Nile doesn't meet my eyes. "I want to go to restaurants."

"Then what do you need to do?"

"Behave."

"Behave," I repeat. "What does that mean? Does that mean you should go back to your seat and lie down across it and kick at the wall?"

Nile's breathing speeds up, and he appears to be on the verge of tears. "I'm ashamed," he says.

"You don't need to be ashamed of anything." I run my fingers through his hair and kiss the side of his head. "Here, let's finish up eating. What do you want to eat, your pakoras, or your chicken?"

"What I need to do now," Nile says, "is make a poop."

I sigh and smile, then push my plate away and lead him to the back of the restaurant. The bathroom is run-down compared to the dining room, with water-damaged ceiling tiles and a few wire coat hangers dangling randomly from wall hooks. Nile pulls down his pants and sits on the toilet, looking me unembarrassed in the eye while I stand there waiting for him to finish.

"I'm done," he announces after a minute. Then he climbs off, stands facing the toilet, grabs hold of the seat with both hands, and sticks his little-boy ass up in the air, waiting for me to wipe him. At school, he wipes himself, but he comes home smelling like a walking butt, and we still take care of it for him at home.

When I've finished wiping him, I walk him to the sink and help him get soap out of the dispenser and wash his hands. There aren't any paper towels, and I wave my hand under the automatic drier and try to get Nile to use it, but he cowers away, backing up toward the door like a nervous dog. He doesn't like the noise.

We're about to get back on the road, and so, even though I don't really have to go, I unzip and take a leak. The hand drier shuts off, and I hear Nile making little noises with his mouth behind me. I turn to look over my shoulder and see him making faces at his own reflection in the round brass doorknob. "I love you,' he whispers.

I shake off into the dingy toilet bowl and zip up. "I love you, too."

• • •

Almost immediately after we get back on the road, we stumble upon a car show on the lawn of something called the Hebert Candy Mansion. We really ought to get some more miles under our tires before Nile's bedtime, but these random little surprises are the whole point of a road trip, and so we pull over and get out of the Black Racer to poke around. I've never cared about cars, and to me the event is just a bunch of middle-aged dudes wandering around, envying of each others' Camaros while "Wooly Bully" plays over the PA. But Nile bounds from car to car with high knees and exaggerated elbows, peeking inside the engines of the ones with raised hoods. I ask him which car is his favorite, and he says, "They're all my favorite!"

A sprinkling of rain ends the event early, and I shepherd Nile back to the Black Racer, indulging him too many times when he asks again and again to watch "just one more" of the classic cars drive away.

Beyond Worcester, the businesses lining the side of the road thin out a bit. The strip malls are replaced by strip clubs, places with names like Centerfolds and Lamplighter II. The traffic finally eases up, either because of the time of day or because we've broken free from Boston's orbit, and I'm able to drive faster than fifty miles per hour for the first time all day. Darkness falls quickly, and when we pull over for our first gas stop, it's pitch black outside.

Nile has been pestering me all summer to let him help me pump gas, but we're always in a hurry to get somewhere, and I've been putting him off, telling him he can help on the way to Iowa. "You ready?" I ask, unbuckling my seatbelt.

"I'm ready," Nile replies from the backseat. "I'll make sure not to start an exploding fire."

"Yeah." I laugh and shake my head, unsure where he's gotten this particular idea. "Definitely make sure not to start an exploding fire."

I get him out of the car, and we stand in the moth-filled light beneath the canopy. I run my credit card, then show Nile how to push the button for regular unleaded and help him insert the nozzle into the tank of the Black Racer. Nile tries to press in the nozzle trigger, but his grip isn't strong enough, and so I put my hand over his and squeeze, and we fill up the tank together.

Earlier, I promised him both the McDonald's milkshake and an ice cream cone at the car show, but we didn't end up getting either, and now I let him come inside with me to pick out a treat. Nile selects a box of Junior Mints (which he calls "candy mints"), and I grab a Diet Mountain Dew to help keep me awake. It's already past Nile's usual eight o'clock bedtime, and as we pull away from the station, I start looking for motels. "Thanks for helping me pump the gas," I say. "You're a pretty big boy."

"I'm glad I didn't make an exploding fire."

"Me too," I say. "Are you having a good day with Daddy?"

"Yes." Nile shakes a Junior Mint into his mouth. "I'm having a good day."

"What's your favorite part of the road trip so far?"

Nile answers instantly. "My favorite part was helping you pump the gas."

"Really?" I'm surprised he didn't name the car show or the Indian restaurant. "Why did you want to help me pump the gas?"

"Because I want to be just like you."

Nile says this casually, as though it's the most obvious thing in the world, but it catches me off guard, like a pinprick to the heart. I know he loves me, but he's never said anything quite like this before, and I have to blink to hold back tears.

The truth is, I don't want him to be just like me. I want him to be better.

"That was a nice thing to say," I tell him, my voice a little uneven. "Hey, you want to know something? Do you want to know one reason I'm taking this trip with you?"

"Why?" Nile asks.

"Because," I tell him. "It's very, very, very, very, very, very, very important to me to be the best daddy that I can be for you."

"Oh," Nile says, chewing his candy. "Well, did you ever go on a trip like this with your daddy when you were a little boy?"

"No," I say, and then the words are out of my mouth before I can stop them: "I don't love my daddy."

Until this moment, I've never spoken to Nile about my father, and he's never asked. Once, they talked on the phone, but it wasn't something I planned, and Nile doesn't remember it. During the winter when Nile was two years old, I called my Grandma Wilson (my father's mother) to let Nile wish her a happy birthday. My father lives rent-free in her basement in Waterloo, and when my Grandma Wilson heard Nile talking in complete sentences for the first time, she said, thrilled, "Rick, pick up the line and listen to this!" I would have hung up, but she's started having memory problems, and it was her birthday, and so instead I listened in on the speaker and heard my father chuckle as my son experimented with subjects and verbs in his inexpert little toddler voice.

It's the only time I've heard my father's voice in the past twelve years.

"You don't love your daddy?" Nile asks me. "Why not?

"Well," I start, unsure if I should even be talking with him about this. I don't want to burden my five-year-old son with my baggage. "He's not very nice."

"Why is he not nice?" Nile asks. "If you say hello to him, does he not say hello back to you? Is that what he does?"

I smile to myself at Nile's innocence. He wants a simple explanation, and the worst scenario he can dream up is that my father is slightly impolite. The truth is a long story, and Nile is too young to understand most of it, but the essence of it is this: My father was almost never around, and when he was around, he was terrible.

I try to put it in terms that Nile can understand. "My daddy didn't play with me," I tell him. "When I was a little boy, I wanted someone to play baseball and hide-and-seek with, and to ride bikes with me, and he didn't do those things."

"Awww," Nile says. "That's sad! I'm glad that you play with me."

I swallow to steady my voice. "I'm glad that I play with you, too, baby."

• • •

I'm oddly excited, pulling the Black Racer into the cramped lot of the Wedgewood Motel, a squat, one-story dive with only ten or twelve rooms. It's been years since I've stayed at a dumpy independent motel, and the place reminds me of the solo road trips I took during college when I didn't have any money, and I would sometimes pay under twenty dollars for rooms that looked like they hadn't been cleaned since the last time someone was murdered in them.

I park in front of the office and pop in, leaving Nile in the car. After a few seconds, a short, trim man with a mustache comes out from another room and tells me there's a room available. I tell him to wait a minute, and then I bring Nile in so I can fill out the paperwork and get our keys. Nile is exhausted, and he bounces around on the carpet, somehow still full of nervous energy that he needs to release, like a car sputtering and shaking before it finally runs out of gas.

"How old?" the man asks, handing me a form to sign. On the countertop sits a ceramic turtle, next to a snow globe with a cardinal locked inside, and a small, square sign that says, "If you ever get caught sleeping at work, just slowly raise your head and say 'In Jesus' name I pray.'"

"Five," I say. "Starting kindergarten in a few weeks."

The man appraises Nile's lanky limbs. "Big for his age. You don't smoke, do you?"

I shake my head.

"Didn't think so." He runs my credit card and hands me a receipt. "Hardly any of the younger people smoke. When I was in high school, you could get your parents to sign a permission form and smoke on your lunch break."

I ask him whether I should bother with Route 20 again in the morning, and he advises me to get back on the interstate. "Route 20 is all stop-and-go," he says.

I thank him and take Nile to the room and set him up with a snack, and then I pull the Black Racer over twenty feet into our designated parking spot and join him. There are two queen beds, a nightstand, a mini-fridge, a large desk, and a generous round dining table, and yet the room is still strangely too large for its furnishings. There's enough space between the bathroom and the beds to park a Mack truck. Outside, it's begun to cool down, but the wall-mounted air conditioner hums loudly, struggling to keep up with the sheer square footage of the space.

Nile and I briefly FaceTime with Belzie, and although she cheerfully asks him about our evening, I can hear a note of worry in her voice. This is the first time Nile has been away from her for more than a night. When I told her I wanted to take this trip with him, she didn't push back against the idea, but she wasn't exactly enthusiastic about it, either. "I love you!" she says, waving goodbye into the phone. "Have fun!" There's something forced about it, like she's forgetting to breathe.

After the call, I get Nile's teeth brushed and do his bedtime. Belzie has packed four or five sets of pajamas, but Nile wants to sleep in his clothes, and I don't fight him. I've brought along a book called "Teach Your Child to Read in 100 Easy Lessons," and I'm hoping to finish it with him before school starts, but there's no way he'll make it through a lesson tonight, and so instead I read him a chapter from the second book in the "Boxcar Children" series. As we lie in bed reading, he gets overtired and antsy, wrestling with the blankets and pressing his feet into my back.

I hurry to finish the chapter and then go through the rest of our nighttime routine. I sing "You Are My Sunshine," and I count to twelve. Then I ask him the same two questions I ask him every night, but he's too exhausted to come up with anything but the most unimaginative possible answers.

"What was your favorite part of the day, baby?" I ask him.

"My favorite part of the day was the trip to Iowa."

I rub his back. "What are you going to dream about?"

Nile's eyes are already closed. "I'm going to dream about

being in this motel."

I kiss him on the top of the head and stand up to use the bathroom, and when I come back, he's already fast asleep. I change into my pajamas and get into the other bed, grabbing the remote control from the nightstand. But before I turn on the television, I stop and close my eyes for a moment, and I let the day play over again in my mind. I think back to the conversation about how I don't love my father. *Why did I bring that up?*

I consider that maybe this wasn't just a pathetic attempt to unburden myself on my five-year-old. Maybe I was trying, unconsciously, to show Nile that I'm a real person with real problems, and not just someone putting on a show where I play the part of the Perfect Dad. I work hard to make Nile see me as someone who can fix anything, who eats healthily and has his life in order, who loves to exercise. I work hard to make him see me as someone who *doesn't* occasionally walk around in public muttering "I hate myself" and hoping that no one hears. But I wonder how much of this is really me trying to set a good example, and how much might be my fear of letting him see the real me.

I want to be for my children the father I never had: present, sober, responsible, hard-working, competent, loving, organized, attentive. And, even when I fall short, I want Nile and Peanut to *think* that's who I am. In a way, they're the ultimate observers of me. When I was a teenager, I believed deeply in God, but by now, I've more or less completely lost my religion, and having children is the closest I ever expect to get to eternity. Absent God, Nile and Peanut will render the final judgment on my life.

One day, all that will be left of me is what my children remember.

Day 2

IT'S HARD FOR ME to talk about my family with strangers.

I don't mean that it's emotionally difficult. If someone asks me what my parents do, I'll often plainly tell them that my mom installs computers at a hospital, and that my dad is a meth addict who lives in his mother's basement. What I mean is that, for the uninitiated, my family is *fucking confusing*. If you're not already familiar with my zigzagging, crisscrossing family tree, you'll never sort it out.

Take my grandparents. I was born with four sets, rather than the usual two, because everybody was already divorced and remarried by the time I came along. There's Papa, my father's father, and Alice, his second wife, who was already divorced, twice from the same man, when she met Papa. I went to live with them when I was eleven, and they adopted me when I was in my teens. This means that, legally, they're my parents, making me my father's brother and my brothers' uncle.

There's my Grandma Wilson, my father's mother, and my Grandpa Wilson, her second husband, who was also already married and divorced when they met. Since they were married before I was born, I grew up knowing Grandpa Wilson's biological grandchildren as my cousins, even though we weren't related by blood. When I was in college, one of them shot his own mother and stepfather to death, and although I was shocked, I felt oddly disconnected from the events. I'd never even met the victims. Hallmark doesn't make a card for when your cousin-by-divorce murders your father's mother's husband's son's ex-wife and her second husband.

There's Oompa, my mom's father, and Madge, his second wife. I believe she was also previously married and divorced, but I'm honestly not really sure. She never liked any of us, and she remarried six months after Oompa died.

And there's my Grandma Jo, my mother's mother, and her live-in boyfriend Scott. Jo and Scott were together for decades, but they never married, because Grandma Jo didn't want to give up the alimony she was still receiving from Oompa. Scott happened to be, through a previous marriage and divorce, the biological grandfather of two of my cousins, and so he was both their paternal grandfather and their maternal step-grandfather.

It's not an exaggeration to say that divorce is the organizing principle in my family. My mother and father divorced before I turned four, and all but one of their six brothers and sisters are divorced. (Even Oompa's and Grandma Jo's fathers walked out on them back in the 1930s, making them divorce pioneers of sorts.) Through all of the divorces and remarriages, I've gained dozens of quasi-cousins and sort-of-aunts and step-grandmother's-niece's-husbands – people who aren't really related to me, but aren't really *not* related to me, either.

It's hard to even keep the basic facts straight. Untangling the feelings is harder.

• • •

The air conditioner, which has been running all night, finally catches up with the motel room, and the icy air wakes me a little after six o'clock in the morning. I try to be quiet in the bathroom, but when I come back out, Nile is stirring and stretching. Most mornings at home, he crawls into bed with Belzie and me, worming his way under the covers, tossing and turning and stabbing his elbows and knees into our sides until we wake up. Today, I crawl into his bed, cuddling up with his bony little body, and kiss the back of his head.

"Is it daytime?" he asks.

"Not yet."

Nile rubs at his eyes. "But it's not nighttime still."

"Maybe it's bite-time," I say.

"What?"

"Kite-time." I kiss his head again. "It's time to make a kite."

"Noooo!" Nile says, catching on now that we're being silly. "It's not kite-time!"

I hop out of bed and lift the blackout curtain on our one small window. It's rained overnight. The sky is a slate gray, and the rental car and the asphalt are a wet, inky black. I try to get Nile to shower in the cramped stall, but he's afraid of the water splashing down onto his face, and so instead I set him up with a strawberry Nutri-Grain bar and a box of chocolate milk, letting him watch television while I load up the car. He settles on a PBS live-action show called "Odd Squad," where kids in business suits walk around solving mysteries that apparently hinge on their ability to identify symmetrical shapes and make 35 cents using different combinations of coins.

"I want to stay here," Nile whines when the show is over.

I survey the spartan room. I don't yet know what today has in store for us, but it has to be better than this. "No, no," I say. "Time to go."

The motel office isn't open yet, and so I leave the key in the room with the door unlocked, and then we're off in the Black Racer. "I did not smoke any cigarettes last night,"

Nile says, remembering the manager's instructions. "Not this morning, either."

I flip on the radio and start scanning for a station. Around Boston, I mostly listen to audiobooks or NPR, but when I'm on a road trip, I like to seek out local stations to get a flavor of wherever I'm driving. Most television content is fairly standardized, produced to be acceptable to the broadest possible audience, but local radio has largely retained its quirkiness, and it can be fascinating to drive along the highway while two grown men work themselves up to the verge of simultaneous heart attacks because someone insulted the Auburn football team, or some really intense, earnest weirdoes talk about Bible-based strategies for disciplining your "strong-willed" child.

I land on a morning show where three men are discussing politics. Last night was the final evening of the Democratic National Convention, and I stayed up and watched Hillary Clinton's speech while Nile slept. She's normally not a natural campaigner, but I thought her speech was warm and optimistic, especially compared with Donald Trump's doom-and-gloom address from the week before.

"You know what?" asks one of the radio hosts. "You know what every man in America heard when they were listening to that speech? Here's what they heard: *Yappity yappity yappity yappity yappity TAKE THE TRASH OUT!*"

"Jesus," I mutter, and click off the radio.

"What?" Nile asks.

"Um." I try not to foist my political views on Nile, although he's decided for himself that he doesn't like Donald Trump "because he says mean words." "These men on the radio were being sexist."

"What's that?" Nile asks.

"It means that they think women aren't as good as men."

"That's not nice." Nile's voice is serious, verging on angry. "Men and women are both good. Not only men can be firefighters. Women can be firefighters, too. And they can even be bus drivers if they want!"

I laugh at his example. "What about president? Can a woman be president?"

"Yes," Nile says. "And that was not a funny joke on the radio. The man was laughing about that women can't do as much as men, and that is not a funny joke!"

♦ ♦ ♦

There's nothing to see on I-90, but the plain green ditches aren't any worse than the endless stream of Burger Kings from yesterday, and at least today I have the sensation that we're moving forward. As we speed past Springfield, I see a sign for the Basketball Hall of Fame. It's probably not open yet, and I don't really care about seeing it, but it gives me an idea. I've wanted to go to the Baseball Hall of Fame in Cooperstown, New York since I was a little kid, and I get a little excited when I look up directions on my phone and discover that it's only twenty miles off the interstate.

I haven't thought about the Hall in years, except for a few days each summer when a new class is inducted, and the sports talking heads all argue about the merits of advanced metrics and speculate on who did or didn't use steroids. I don't watch baseball anymore, and I quit playing in the fifth grade, but when I was a little boy, it was everything to me. I had zero athletic ability, and no father to coach me along, but I was convinced that I would one day pitch in the major leagues. My hero was Nolan Ryan, a fireball-throwing Texan who was in his mid-forties and nearing retirement by the time I was old enough to pay attention. His game depended on his fastball, and he was famous for striking batters out with pitches that clocked in above a hundred miles per hour. At his age, this sort of velocity required an exaggerated wind-up, where he would kick his front leg high up in the air in front of him, nearly kneeing himself in the nose before he hurled the ball toward home plate.

If I ever had any chance of being a decent pitcher, it died with my attempt to copy Nolan Ryan's delivery. At eight years old, I didn't possess the timing necessary for my leg kick to add any oomph to my pitches, and instead I was just wildly erratic. I really did work at it. My Uncle Mark drew a life-sized catcher in Sharpie on a white bedsheet, and I would string it up in our backyard and practice my fastball for hours. Like a true nerd, I even went to the library and checked out books on pitching mechanics. But when I asked my Little League coach if I could try out to be a pitcher, he only let me throw two errant pitches before deciding he'd seen enough and stashing me in right field.

I always thought the reason I was a terrible athlete was because all the other boys had fathers and I didn't, and I assumed that Nile would fare better with me around. But he's just not very interested in sports, and has no competitive instincts. Last summer, a group of older boys let him play in a soccer game, and he ran around the field with them, shrieking and laughing. But when I called out, "Nile, kick the ball!" he answered, "Somebody's already kicking it!"

"Nile," I say now, trying to meet his eyes for a moment in the rearview mirror. "What do you know about baseball?"

"I know nothing about baseball," Nile answers.

"Well, you've got two hours to learn everything," I tell him. "We're going the Hall of Fame. It's a place where they have pictures of all of the best baseball players, and you can see their hats, and their bats, and the uniforms they wore."

I realize that I'm not selling this any better than I did the rodeo, and I try again. "I've always wanted to go, but I never did, and now I'm going to go with you. Are you excited?"

I expect Nile to maybe whine about how he'd rather go to another car show, but instead he says, "I'm excited."

"You are?" I ask. "Why are you excited?"

"Because I get to be with you."

I launch into an impromptu survey course on the history of baseball, rattling off the names of the greats: Babe Ruth, Hank Aaron, Ted Williams, Mickey Mantle, Willie Mays. But for every player I mention, I end up going through a rabbit hole of explanations. Babe Ruth hit more home runs than anyone else at the time, I tell Nile, but then I have to explain what a home run is. I tell him that Nolan Ryan recorded more strikeouts than any other pitcher, but he doesn't know what a strikeout is, or a strike, or a ball, or a foul tip.

"Did you get three strikes, Daddy?" Nile asks, trying out his new understanding of the rules.

"I got three strikes almost every time I came to the plate," I tell him. I remember hitting the ball out of the infield exactly once, but I got too excited and tried to stretch the hit into a double, and I was out by a mile at second base.

"So that means you had to sit down."

"Yep," I say. "Three strikes and you're out."

"That's not very fair."

"It's fair," I say. "It's the same rules for everybody. I just wasn't very good at hitting the ball."

"Maybe if I was your father, I would help you," Nile says. "Maybe then you could hit the ball."

• • •

We pull off for gas at a truck stop, where Nile practices his reading on the bathroom stall graffiti ("D-A-L-E. Dale? Does that say Dale?"). I get him a strawberry donut with sprinkles at the Dunkin Donuts counter and order myself an iced coffee with whole milk, still trying to stay away from sugar. Every couple of minutes, a man's voice comes over the PA to tell a trucker that his shower stall is ready, and I briefly try to imagine what it must be like to spend sixteen hours a day behind the wheel of a big rig. My father drove trucks for a while when I was little, I think, but he didn't stick with it long. He's never stuck with anything for very long.

Nile has heavy lids and tired, watery eyes, and when he's finished with his donut, he comes and sits on my lap in a near-vegetative state, watching the rotating digital menu of colorful Dunkin Donuts Coolattas. I rub his back, all knotty muscle and bony spine, and he squirms in my arms, full again of that tired, anxious energy.

Back in the car, Nile perks up a bit, inventing a game where we say "HONK!!!" as loud as we can whenever we see a big rig. This gets old nearly instantly, and we switch to his new game, pretending that we're two firefighters named Buck and Biff, speeding down the road on our way to various emergencies.

We end up back on Route 20 for a bit, and this stretch is much nicer than the one leading out of the Boston suburbs, more bucolic, with little antique shops popping up every couple of miles. The sun has emerged from behind the clouds, and the hillsides and hayfields are lit up a bright green. Wildflowers grow in the ditches, and the roadside is dotted with pretty country homes, but also, confusingly, with some of the most bombed-out looking houses and barns I've ever seen – structures with 30-degree leans and Volvo-sized holes in their roofs. It's as though the area has undergone some sort of regional mini-apocalypse, and while the landscape has regenerated and the citizens have rebuilt, they've left up the war-torn buildings as a grim warning to future generations.

"Daddy," Nile says. "Will you tell me more about baseball?"

"Sure, baby," I say. "What do you want to know?"

"Tell me more about the old-fashioned players."

"Let me think. Did you ever hear of Jackie Robinson?"

"No, Daddy," Nile says. "Who's he?"

Up to now, I've almost completely avoided discussing racism – or even race at all – with Nile. I know it's something that will affect his life, but I also strongly feel that it's just *not his problem*, at least not yet. He's five years old. Until a year ago, he described people as "blue" or "gray" or "purple," depending on the color of their shirt they were wearing. Recently, he's begun noticing differences in skin color, but his descriptions are childlike and precise, and have nothing to do with the over-simplified labels and complex histories that inform grown-up conversations about race. Nile says that he's "tannish," that Belzie is "brownish," and that I am "kind of pinkish." He notices that Belzie has braids, that my hair is straight, and that he and Peanut have curls. It hasn't occurred to him – because why would it? – that anyone might use these distinctions as an excuse to treat some people differently from others.

It's impossible right now to know what sort of impact race will have on Nile's sense of identity, or how it will circumscribe his ability to move through the world as he pleases. It is my whitest, most naive hope that my son will never have to worry about racism at all. I hope that we'll make progress quickly enough that racism won't affect him, or that he'll be light-skinned enough that it won't affect him, or that he'll always be well-dressed and well-spoken enough for it not to affect him. I make up all sorts of reasons – the diversity of our community, the liberal politics of our state – that racism won't touch my son in the way it's touched virtually every person of color who's ever lived in America.

Belzie has no such illusions. She's certain that, in just a few years, we'll need to have difficult conversations with Nile about how other people may see his skin color and his gender and perceive him as a threat. She's certain that we'll have to tell him not to play hide-and-seek after dark, so that he's not mistaken for a burglar; that we'll have to tell him to keep his hands visible when he's in a store, so that he's not mistaken for a thief; that we'll have to teach him to move slowly and say *yessir* and *nossir* when he interacts with police, so that he's not mistaken for someone who must be shot before he shoots them.

I hope she's wrong. I doubt that she is.

"Nile," I say. "Do you know what 'white people' and 'black people' mean?"

It makes me a little sad to even use the words with him. It feels like I'm deliberately peeling away a layer of his innocence.

"What?" Nile says. "What's that?"

"People that look like Mommy are called 'black people,'" I tell him. "And people that look like Daddy are called 'white.'"

"Oh," Nile says. "Am I white? Or am I black?"

I pause. The obvious answer to this question is: "Both." The more nuanced answer is: "Throughout history, many men who you would call 'pinkish' raped women you would call 'brownish,' so that lots of people who are considered 'black' today probably have less African blood in them than you do; and anyway, for much of this country's history, white people have subscribed to something called the 'one-drop rule,' which would classify not only you as black, but also your children, and their children, on into infinity; and these definitions and categories seem to be shifting, although it's unclear to me exactly what is changing, or for whom, or how quickly; but, after hundreds of years of treating skin color as the most important thing in the world, many white people suddenly don't want to hear anything about it, and will, if you vocalize your thoughts about race and identity for more than a few seconds, ask you *what the big deal is* or why you're so *obsessed with race*; and although overt discrimination is certainly less frequent today than it was fifty years ago, this does not mean that racism is over, but rather that racism has largely retreated deep into the subconscious minds of most white people, a part that they – I mean "we," this applies to me, too – have walled off with the words I'M NOT RACIST; and whether you're a black boy or a white boy is going to be determined more by how other people perceive you than any label you apply to yourself; and to the extent that people perceive you as 'black,' many of them will also perceive you as 'scary'; and even though you're the one scaring them, it's you who will be in danger."

Instead of giving him either of these answers, I say, "Well, you think you're 'tannish,' right?"

"Yeah," Nile replies. "I'm pretty much tannish."

"A long time ago," I tell him, "people who looked like Mommy and people who looked like Daddy weren't allowed to play together on the same baseball teams. What do you think of that idea?"

"I don't think that's good," Nile says. "That's not fair!"

"That's right, baby," I tell him. "It's important to treat people fairly, but that's not what happened. The black people had to make their own baseball teams. Those teams had some really great players, like Josh Gibson and Satchel Paige, but they weren't allowed to play on the same teams as the white players. And the first black player who got to play on a white team was named Jackie Robinson."

"Jackie Robinson," Nile repeats.

"A lot of people didn't want him to play with the white people," I say. "They were mean to him."

Nile gasps, almost comically. "That's not what you should do! Even if you're angry, you should use your words."

"They did use their words, baby," I tell him. "But the words they used were really mean."

"WHAT?!?!?" Nile says. "Did they use words like 'stupid'?"

"The words they used were even meaner than that."

"Like 'shut up'? Did they say 'shut up'?"

"Yeah, baby," I say, not ready to tell Nile about actual ugliness of the history. "They told him to shut up."

"That's not good," Nile says. "I don't like that."

"I know, baby," I say. "But you don't have to worry about it now. Black people and white people can play on the same baseball teams. And it's because of Jackie Robinson."

There's a falseness to what I'm telling him, this implication that racism is something from the past, something we've dealt with and moved on from. It's the way I learned about racism in school when I was a kid: *We used to do this bad thing, and then we stopped.* But, of course, that's not the story of race in America at all. What would I even tell him, if I thought he was ready to hear the truth? Would I say that black kids and white kids are allowed to go to the same schools now, but they almost never do, because every time black people move into a neighborhood, all the white people sell their houses, and there's no way to make a law against that? Would I tell him that there's an entire world of opportunities open to him, but that he also has to watch out if he gets a summer tan and wears a hooded sweatshirt and walks home from the store in the dark, because then someone might follow him down the street and shoot him, and not only will the killer get away with it, but people will make *shooting targets* that look like him, so they can gleefully pretend to murder him all over again?

After a few minutes of silence, Nile pipes up again from the back seat. "Daddy? Could I play on the baseball team?"

"You can play on whatever team you want," I assure him. "There aren't any white teams or black teams anymore. Everybody can play together."

"But what about in the old-fashioned days?" he asks. "Would they let me play on the white team then?"

"No, baby," I tell him. "Probably not."

• • •

I'm completely charmed as we roll into Cooperstown. I sort of expected the place to be tacky and overbuilt, like a miniature, baseball-themed version of Las Vegas, but it must have really incredible zoning or something. The main drag downtown still allows head-in parking, and the buildings all top out at three stories, with ground floors populated by souvenir shops with names like Mickey's Place and Shoeless Joe's Hall of Shame. Antique light poles sprout up from the brick sidewalks, hung with red and orange flowers that burst from their baskets like fireworks.

I try to get a good father-son selfie on the steps in front of the Hall, but Nile is tired and squirmy. Of the dozens of photos I take, the best is a shot of me kissing him between his squinty eyes, with an overweight Chicago Cubs fan looking on in the background.

Inside, I take us directly to the Hall of Fame Gallery. There's no memorabilia here, no videos, nothing to tell the story of how the game has evolved over time. It's just three hundred copper plaques stuffed with statistics, like a bricks-and-mortar baseball Wikipedia. When people say that a player has been "enshrined" in the Hall, this is the room they're talking about. It's the room I always imagined visiting when I was a kid.

We walk around, floating to the spots where other people seem to be lingering, and I read the plaques aloud to Nile. Some of the newer ones, for players like Ryne Sandberg and Wade Boggs, are filled with numbers: how many games in a row they went without making a fielding error, how many years they led the league in runs, their postseason batting averages, their precise career totals for hits and walks and stolen bases. But the plaque dedicated to Babe Ruth simply says: *Greatest drawing card in history of baseball. Holder of many home run and other batting records. Gathered 714 home runs in addition to fifteen in World Series.* Something about this approach feels more legendary, more sepia-tinted, as though Ruth played at a time when facts were merely whispers, and no numbers could possibly tell you anything about how great he truly was.

I make a point of stopping by Jackie Robinson's plaque. The text begins with descriptions of his play, lauding his "extraordinary ability" and "electrifying style," then goes into a few sentences about his stats before concluding with: *Displayed tremendous courage and poise in 1947 when he integrated the modern major leagues in the face of intense adversity.* I'll find out later that this is a new plaque, unveiled less than a decade ago, and that this final sentence never appeared on the original. When Jackie Robinson first became eligible for the Hall, he asked that voters only consider him on the merits of his play, and not take his status as a civil rights hero into account.

After we're done with the gallery, we speed through the

rest of the exhibits. If I were here alone, I would linger for hours, but Nile is getting tired, and I settle for quick glimpses of Babe Ruth's uniform and Honus Wagner's cleats. We pass a television playing a video of a bench-clearing brawl, and I immediately recognize it as the time when umpires incorrectly reversed a George Brett home run because he had too much of a foreign substance on his bat.

"Why are they fighting?" Nile asks. "Is it because a black man wanted to play on the white team?"

"No, baby," I tell him. "They're fighting about pine tar."

Eventually, we follow our museum map to something called the Sandlot Kids' Clubhouse. I've been imagining it as a large space filled with puzzles and coloring activities and maybe even a baseball-themed jungle gym, but it's just a small room in a back corner with a few picture books. We're about to leave when a man in a museum uniform stops us and tells us that some outdoor baseball activities for kids will begin in a few minutes.

Nile and I step outside onto a little lawn. There are a few other kids already waiting, all of them at least a year or two older than Nile. A few weeks ago, I took him to a field day at a park near our house on the Fourth of July. Nile's no athlete, but he's a good runner, and when he was four years old, he once jogged three miles straight while I panted along beside him, struggling to keep up. But on the field day, Nile became overwhelmed by the crowd and refused to line up and race the other boys, who all seemed so carefree and happy. I had to carry him away from the park while he whimpered and pouted, hiding his face in my shoulder.

Which is to say, I do not have high hopes for this.

The coach, a tall, fit man, dark-skinned man in his early twenties, starts the kids out with some basic stretching: toe touches, arm windmills. Nile keeps up a running commentary, denigrating his own abilities and praising the efforts of the other kids. "Ugh, I can't do his!" he shouts. And then: "Oh, you're trying so hard!"

Next, the coach tosses the kids some gentle ground balls. Waiting in line, Nile jumps up and down, cheering the other kids on, but when it's his turn, he motions for the boy behind him to go instead. The coach coaxes Nile into participating, and he throws his little body on top of the grounders, giggling as he tosses them back. I didn't realize it until now, but I've been holding my breath a little this whole time, and now I finally let it out. I don't care whether Nile is any good at sports. I just want him to have fun.

The kids take turning sprinting out and back to a series of cones, each placed a little farther from the starting line than the last. These were called "suicides" when I was a kid, but they must have been renamed by now. Nile is surprisingly terrible at this. He can chug along at a jogging pace forever, but when he sprints, his limbs end up all over the place, and anyway he's laughing and doesn't even seem to realize that he's supposed to be running fast. "Last cone, last cone!" the coach says in his rah-rah voice. Nile ambles to the last cone, touches it delicately with the tip of one finger as though trying not to knock it over, and slowly makes his way back down the homestretch. "Niiiiiiice," the coach says. "I like it."

When they're done, the coach gives each of the kids a four-pack of baseball cards for participating. Nile hands me his prize and then runs off with the other children, who all chase each other around bronze statues of a catcher and a pitcher. "We're not in New York City!" Nile tells a blond kid in an orange tee shirt. "I've never been inside the Statue of Liberty!"

"Well," the blond kid responds. "I'm six years old!"

"I'm five and a half," Nile says. "So I'm almost six."

"Well I'm already six," the boy answers. "So I'm way older than you."

Nile searches for something to come back at the kid with, but he doesn't really know how to be mean, and so he just throws his arms back and puffs his chest out and shouts, as loud as he can, "HA HA!!!" In a minute, though, they're friends again, discussing whether or not the insect at my feet is a ladybug.

Gradually, all the other kids leave, and Nile is by himself, sucking wind and sweating. "Oh," he whines. "I wish we had told them where we live. Then maybe we could have a playdate."

"We're going to meet lots of new friends on this trip," I tell him. "We won't see most of them again."

"That's not very nice."

"Don't be sad," I say. "Just tell your friends goodbye."

"Bye, guys!" Nile calls out to the blond boy and his brother, who are walking away with their parents. "I'm glad for playing with you!"

They give a noncommittal "yep" and keep walking.

. . .

Nile and I wander in and out of a few of the shops on the main drag, hunting for souvenirs. The pleasure centers of my addict's brain light up at the sight of all the cheap baseball cards, which I collected voraciously in the late 1980s and early 1990s, when the baseball card bubble (a real thing that somehow existed in the world) was just about to burst. Papa, my father's father, got me into collecting. He claimed that he'd once owned the rare and famous Honus Wagner card that routinely commanded high-six-figure prices at auction. His story didn't add up. The T206 Honus Wagner was produced and inserted into packages of cigarettes in 1909, more than two decades before Papa was even born. He must have pulled a reprint out of a pack of gum when he was a kid. Still, he went to his grave thinking he'd just missed out on striking it rich.

Papa had a bad shoulder and couldn't play catch with me, but he took me to a couple of major league games, and he drove me around from one baseball card shop to another, scouting and scooping up potential investments. He had two years of junior college and retired as a vice president at a bank in Des Moines, but I can see now that he never had any special insight into money. He was convinced that these baseball cards – all of them virtually worthless now – would one day make me rich, all because of that phantom Honus Wagner card. We would buy packs of Donruss, Topps, Score, and Upper Deck, and then spend hours organizing the cards into nine-pocket sleeves in three-ring binders. Today, they're all sitting in Alice's basement in Waterloo.

My father never took me to a game, but he did occasionally send my brothers and me game-used baseballs after we moved to Rockport with our mom. He would go to the Waterloo minor league ballpark and game days and stand outside the gates, waiting for players to ding foul balls into the parking lot, and then he would try to out-scramble the other ballhawks for the souvenir. After he'd collected five or six balls, he would box them up and ship them out to us in Massachusetts, along with pocketknives he'd purchased with Marlboro Miles and strips of dried glue drippings from the factory where he was working, which he thought looked neat for some reason. The gesture is sort of undeniably sweet and desperate and a little pathetic, and yet, I'm unable to appreciate it. I'm thirty-four years old, and the best thing my father has done for me since I was born is send me baseballs and glue drippings in the mail. If that's the best I could do for Nile in a single day, I would be ashamed of myself. When I think of those baseballs, all long since lost in the tall grasses and woodlands that surrounded the sandlots where I played as a child, I don't think: Well, at least he tried. What I think is: What a piece of shit.

Inside one of the Cooperstown shops, I let Nile pick out a souvenir. At first, he wants one of the wildly overpriced knockoff Lego baseball sets, but he eventually selects a baseball from a bin of balls that have been used in spring training, and I let him grab a box of 1983 player stickers, too. On our way to the register, unable to resist, I grab a couple packages of 1990 Upper Deck baseball cards, and I feel the same giddy tingle of anticipation that I felt buying a new pack of cards when I was eight years old.

Nile and I take our souvenirs to a small, crowded diner across the street and find two seats at the counter. Nile claims not to be hungry, but my burger turns out to be fourteen ounces, and when it comes, he shares it with me and eats most of my fries. While we eat, he opens his box of stickers, which, like each of my packs of baseball cards, was priced at a single measly dollar. The stickers, only a year younger than I am, are coiled and ruined at the bottoms of their strips, but the tops are okay, and Nile peels them from their paper and pastes them back onto their own box. I tear away the foil wrapping on my cards and find mostly players I don't remember at all, but also Hall of Famer Paul Molitor and All-Star Orel Hershiser, along with a rookie card for slugger Juan Gonzalez. The haul would have made me plenty happy back in 1990, and even now I experience a momentary little high, but then I'm left with thirty pieces of cardboard and nothing to do with them.

After lunch, we stop to peek inside Doubleday Field, where two teams of teenagers are playing in what appears to be some sort of scrimmage. The uniforms don't all match, and the players honestly aren't all that good, and although the stadium seats nearly ten thousand fans, Nile and I are among only a few dozen people in attendance, all of us huddled in the shade of the roof behind home plate. It's Nile's first baseball game of any sort, and I take the opportunity to talk him through balls and strikes, the infield and the outfield, stolen bases and pop flies. The rest of the spectators are lackadaisical in their support, but Nile exclaims "Oh!" and "Awwww!" and "Yeah!" at random moments. "Why isn't anyone else clapping?" he asks me. Before I can answer, he shouts down to the batter, "You can do this!"

We only stay for an inning. It's mid-afternoon, and we should get back on the road and try to make some progress before we settle in for the night. On our way out of town, I drive the Black Racer over a bridge with a tiny water spillover underneath it, and Nile asks me to stop the car. "I want to see the waterfall."

I've been thinking about where to drive next, and I take this as a sign. "We don't have time to stop," I tell him. "But if you want to see a waterfall, I know where to find a good one."

· · ·

We sit at the border, waiting to cross. And sit. And sit.

The Black Racer has been inching alongside what must be the world's largest Days Inn here on the American side of Niagara Falls for the better part of an hour, but the actual border checkpoint is nowhere in sight. I've already booked a prepaid room on the Canadian side of the Falls, using my laptop at a travel plaza about ninety miles before we hit Buffalo; otherwise, I'd just give up and book a room at the Days Inn.

It can't be full. It's the size of the Death Star.

After Cooperstown, Nile took a long nap in the car, but he's wide awake now, and so I pop in the CD of "The Mouse and the Motorcycle" to keep him occupied. Every couple of minutes, the cars in front of me move forward a few feet, and I let off the brake just a little, and then press down into it again. My leg is cramping, my neck is tense, and I can feel a headache setting in. Before I had kids, this sort of thing would cause me to flail and smack the steering wheel and yell curse words until my voice went hoarse, but Nile's presence in the back seat reminds me that losing my shit won't fix anything. It will only teach him that it's okay to act like a madman when things don't go his way.

As we wait, the sun becomes a big yellow ball on the horizon, and then dips below it, turning the sky shades of purple and pink and orange that would be beautiful if viewed from anywhere other than the inside of a Toyota Avalon that has moved approximately thirteen feet in the past forty-five minutes. And then night settles around us, and our view is just a sea of red taillights, backgrounded by the neon of the hotels across the river.

After two hours, we finally creep up to the booth of a Canadian border agent. For the first time, it occurs to me that bringing Nile across an international border alone, with nothing but my word to suggest that I'm not kidnapping him from an estranged spouse or something, might be a problem.

The agent is a man around my age, but leaner and clean-cut, with impeccable posture. I hand our passports through the window and try to manage a weary smile, but the man just stares back at me, plain-faced.

"Where are you coming from?" he asks. Only, he says it as though it's all one word, with no hint of a question mark at the end. *Whereareyoucomingfrom.*

"Boston," I tell him, then turn to the back seat. "Nile, look at the man so he can see your face."

"WhatareyoudoinginCanada," the agent says. "Howlongareyoustaying."

"Just seeing the Falls," I say, trying too hard to sound casual. "We'll probably stay just the night, maybe two."

The man peers into the car. "That your son with you? Where's mom?"

"She's back in Boston," I tell him. "But actually, she's meeting up with us in Chicago in a few days."

The man's expression changes, and I can tell that this detail sounds, to him, possibly invented. "Whatsthisabout," he demands. "Whyareyoutravelingseparately."

I get a pit in my stomach. I can feel this whole thing heading south. While I don't want to seem evasive, I suspect that it would be a mistake to launch into a whole spiel about our Great American (and Now Canadian, Too!) Road Trip to Discover the Meaning of Modern Manhood. So I try to give him just the bare bones of our itinerary, mentioning that we'll be seeing family and friends in several stops. I think I'm doing well until I get to the end and ramble for far too long about how this is actually a rental car, and we'll be returning it in Des Moines and then flying back to Boston, where of course we'll be reunited again with my wife and daughter.

The man stares unblinking at me for a long moment, and I think that I've been "caught" somehow, that he's going to make me pull over. He's going to call for backup, and search my trunk, and check with the FBI to see if any "tannish" little boys from Boston have been abducted by their disheveled, possibly addled "pinkish" fathers.

Finally, he opens his mouth. "Doyouhaveagun."

"What?" I say, a little too loudly. "I mean, no. No, I definitely don't have a gun."

The agent hands me our passports and waves us away, seemingly bored of listening to me. "Have a nice trip."

· · ·

We get to our hotel just before ten o'clock. The desk clerk, a twenty-something woman named Samantha, is pretty in the same practical, no-frills, almost bureaucratic way that all young women who work at hotel front desks are pretty. Her uniform is crisp, and she wears her long brown hair pulled back into a neat French braid. The traffic is likely due to the fact that this weekend is Canada's Civic Holiday, Samantha tells me, although she's unclear on exactly what this means. "Just an excuse to have a day off, I think. But they're setting off fireworks in a couple of minutes, and you can catch them if you hurry around back. Leave your car out front for now."

I usher Nile through the lobby and out the hotel's rear door, which opens to the parking lot. We stand on the stoop for a minute, and then the fireworks start, just as Samantha promised. They're off in the distance and low to the horizon, just barely clearing the top of the Dumpster that sits in the middle of the parking lot, and I think they must be shooting them from the bottom of the Falls. The views along the river are probably spectacular, with the fireworks lighting up the water.

Belzie and I haven't ever bothered keeping Nile up past his bedtime on the Fourth of July, and so these are his first fireworks. They're far enough away not to be ear-splitting, but the flash-bangs still scare him, and he plugs his ears and turns away at first. But then he talks himself through it with a bizarre bit of little-kid logic. "A fire truck is loud, too, and fire trucks aren't scary," he says. "So this isn't scary, either. Right, Daddy?"

"That's right, baby," I agree, over the pop-pop-pop of the fireworks. "It's not scary."

In just a couple of minutes, the display is over. I'm exhausted, the car needs to be moved, and we still haven't had dinner. The smoke from the fireworks clears in the distance, and I groggily survey the cityscape: the lit-up Ferris wheel, the pyramid-shaped IMAX theatre across the street, the Space Needle knockoff tower stretching up to the sky. And, of course, the Dumpster.

"Oh, Daddy," Nile says, looking out at the same scene. "The city is so beautiful."

Day 3

NILE RARELY SLEEPS LATER than six o'clock, but it's past eight, and still, he's lying lifeless on the plush queen mattress, open-mouthed and drooling. I'm tired, too, and I can't imagine folding myself back up into the Black Racer a few hours from now and sitting in traffic at the border again. I call down to the front desk and book the room for a second night.

"Good news," I say to Nile when he finally stirs awake. "We're staying in Niagara Falls until tomorrow."

Last night, after the fireworks, Nile begged me to stay here an extra day, but now he just gives me an indifferent little grunt, then crawls out of bed and makes his way to the picture window. I help him raise the blackout curtain, and he's surprised to see that the city, which was lit up like a carnival the night before, is now sleepy and gray. Our room faces the rear lot, and the window looks out on the IMAX theater, the Ferris wheel, and the smoke-like mist of the Horseshoe Falls rising up from behind some ugly brick buildings in the distance. Nile sits eating his Nutri-Grain bar and drinking his chocolate milk, entranced by the cityscape.

I call Belzie. She asks me what Nile is having for breakfast, and I can hear her frowning over the phone.

"You should feed him some oatmeal," she says. "He's going to get constipated."

"He's fine," I say. "Trust me. I've spent half of this trip just wiping this kid's ass."

"Still," Belzie insists. "A little oatmeal wouldn't hurt."

"We don't have a microwave in our room," I tell her. "Or milk. Or a refrigerator. Or *oatmeal*."

"Make sure he has a vegetable with lunch, then."

"You know," I say. "For someone who's back in Boston, you're quite literally all up in our shit."

Belzie laughs, but I can tell that she'll want an update tomorrow on the frequency, volume, color, and consistency of Nile's bowel movements.

I'd planned to take Nile on the Hornblower cruise around the Falls this morning, but raindrops being to streak the window as he's eating, and I flip through the glossy attractions guide that I picked up at the front desk, looking for other options. There are half a dozen varieties of miniature golf to choose from, a couple of arcades, and a host of novelty museums. The one thing I want to make sure to do, other than visit the Falls, is ride go-karts at the track outside of town. Nile has been begging me to ride go-karts since he was two years old, and now he's finally old enough. I tear out a coupon for the track and tuck it into my wallet, smiling as I imagine the fun that Nile will have speeding around the turns.

After Nile's done eating, I fish "Teach Your Child to Read in 100 Easy Lessons" out of my bag and sit on the bed with Nile to make our way through Lesson 67. Normally, I resist this sort of direct instruction. I want Nile to learn through play and exploration, and my mom thinks I'm crazy for pushing him to read before kindergarten. But the book is effective, and Nile enjoys sounding out new words and turning them into stories. More to the point, I don't want to send my half-black son to school even a hair behind his white peers. Black boys drop out of school at higher rates than any other group. They have lower grades and test scores. They get suspended more often than anybody else. I want Nile to be a shining star from Day One. I want my actions to communicate, *Listen, you may have some implicit biases and presumptions about the academic trajectory of black boys, and while I'm troubled by that, that isn't what we're talking about right now; we're talking about my son, and my son is DIFFERENT, and if you try to tag him with low expectations or label him a "trou-blemaker," you're going to have to deal with his annoying, involved, middle-class white father who has already taught him how to read.* I may be overthinking things, but I don't care. I can't control everything about the way the world will perceive my son, but I can control this.

Nile slowly sounds out a list of words. *Stop. Come. Teach.* And then I move my index finger under the words as he reads a story about a fat man who steals a car. The stories in this book are all really strange. There's one about a cow who insists he's actually a fish, and another about wealthy pigs who own sailing ships. But I guess that's what happens when you have to write a hundred different stories using kin-dergarten-level sight words.

When we're done, Nile asks me, out of nowhere, "If you were going to get ice cream from an ice cream truck, what would you eat before the ice cream truck comes?"

"Hot dogs," I say, not actually pausing to consider the silly question.

"No," Nile says. "If an ice cream truck was coming to our house, what would you eat first?"

"I'm saying, I would eat hot dogs."

"Oh," he says. "I thought you would say vegetables."

"All right." *Are we playing a game?* I wonder. *Are there rules here?* "Well, I can eat hot dogs *and* vegetables."

Nile laughs and shakes his head. "Oh, no."

"I can't?" I say. "Why not?"

"That's just life," Nile says.

"Hold on," I say. "I need to test something."

"What?"

"Come here," I say. "Come closer to me."

"What is it?"

"I just need to test how comfy this bed is." I snatch Nile up into my arms. Then, carefully but swiftly, I drop him back down onto the pillows, and jump onto the bed with him, tickling the spot just beneath his chin, the one that gets him every time. Nile collapses into giggles and curls up into a ball.

"Is it comfy?" I say.

Nile laughs. "It's comfy!"

"Let me test it again." I stand up and pick Nile up again and toss him back onto the mattress, then flip him over onto his stomach. "You know what?"

"What?" Nile says, panting.

"It's too bad that we're not having any fun."

I tickle the spot under his chin again, and Nile throws his head back in laughter, so that I can see all of his teeth. Between gasps he says, "We are! We are!"

I lie down next to Nile on the bed and put my arm around him. When he sees that I'm done tickling him, his little muscles loosen up, and we lie there for a moment, looking up together at the ceiling.

"Has anybody ever had this much fun?" I ask.

"No," Nile says. "Nobody's ever had this much fun."

• • •

We pad down to the hotel pool, Nile in his water shoes and me in my flip-flops. Even though we won't be out in the sun, he insists on wearing his protective swim shirt. When I was a kid, no one even put sunscreen on me, and my skin would turn lobster-red after hours in the sun, peeling off my shoulders and nose in layers.

The pool here is small, and there aren't any swim toys for Nile to play with, but he can't wait to get in the water. I remember how exciting it was, for some reason, to swim in a hotel pool when I was a boy. I took my very first road trip, if you could call it that, when I was eight years old, and my mom loaded my brothers and me into the car and set off from Iowa to Massachusetts (the very reverse, it occurs to me, of the trip I'm on right now). My mom was running away from my father. He'd lived with us on and off during the years since their divorce, but after my mom kicked him out for good, he went berserk. He would call the house late at night and breathe into the phone. He would break in while we were away and burn cigarette holes into my mom's underwear. My brothers and I were too young to know any of these details yet, and we were just excited by the prospect of staying at a hotel with a swimming pool during the drive out East. The hotel the first night didn't have a pool, but my mom had promised us, and so even though we could have pushed through to Rockport in two days, and even though she didn't have the money to spend, she stopped at a Ramada Inn in Connecticut and let us swim.

I have hardly any memories of my father from the time before we left Iowa. My mom has told me that he refused to help out when we were little. Once, she had to call Papa and Alice over to help with the twins while my father cooked himself a steak dinner. I have a vague, possibly invented, recollection of him drinking a beer and watching television when I was three or four years old and threatening to spank my "bare ass" if I didn't quiet down. I remember coming home sick from second grade one day, and he told me to wake him up if I needed anything, but when I asked him to make me some macaroni and cheese, he didn't rouse from his nap. I remember his crippling addiction to the Nintendo game "The

Legend of Zelda." Once, my mom took my brothers and me to visit Grandma and Grandpa Wilson in Waterloo for the weekend. My father stayed home, and my mom brought the video games with us so we could play them on my cousin's console, but my father thought she'd taken the games out of spite. When we came home, he threw a suitcase across the kitchen, leaving a black streak on the linoleum that never went away.

I can remember a handful of good times, too. Camping. Making snow forts. The way my dad would mix dish soap and water in paint trays and then fashion oversized bubble wands out of wire coat hangers. I remember being with him one day when he was working on some project in the driveway in Maxwell, and I asked him what the purpose of life was, since people were all going to die anyway. "This whole thing is just God's ant farm," he told me. These moments are all just snapshots in my mind, and I have no idea whether they're things that happened only once, or if maybe my father was more involved in our lives when we were little than I give him credit for now.

I think of the endless ocean of days I spend with Nile. I wonder if, years from now, they'll be reduced to a handful of random memories. The thought makes me want to grab hold of the good moments and imprint them onto his brain somehow. I want to tell him, "No matter what happens, remember this time when you were with your daddy, and you were happy."

When my father discovered that we were gone, he didn't call his own father, Papa, to find out where we were. Papa knew where we'd gone, had waved goodbye to us with tears in his eyes as we backed out of the driveway in Maxwell, but by then he was closer with my mom than he was his own son, and he might not have told. My father didn't call his mother, my Grandma Wilson, who may or may not have known where we were, but certainly would have told him if she had. Instead, he went directly to my elementary school, barged into my third-grade classroom, and shouted, "Where's Calvin?!"

A scuzzy little boy named Robert Moore answered, "Massachusetts."

Within a couple of months, my father was there, too, sleeping at first in his car, and then in the spare rooms of a series of booze-soaked Gloucester fishermen. He found work, and although his child support payments were meager and sporadic, he won the right to take my brothers and me out with him on weekends. He barbecued chicken for us one day and took us to see "Batman Returns." Afterward, he told my mom to feed us before we came, since he was short on cash. Then, the next time we saw him, he showed off his expensive new camera. My mom and brothers and I marched in the July 4 Rockport parade, dressed up as "Popeye and Friends." My brother Pete, the smaller of the twins, was Sweet Pea, wearing a bonnet and sitting in a stroller pushed by my mom, who went as Olive Oyl. My dad showed up with the camera, drunk, snapping pictures and slurring, "Hey, Pee Wee!"

Years later, my father and I both ended up back in Iowa: me in Maxwell with Alice; him in Waterloo, first on his own, and then eventually, and permanently, in my Grandma Wilson's basement. We spoke on the phone occasionally, but we didn't have much to talk about. I knew, by now, the stories – the late-night calls, the cigarette holes in the underwear, the lack of child support payments.

"I love you," my father would say when he was ready to hang up the phone.

"Okay," I'd respond.

"Do you love me back?" he'd ask.

"I guess," I would say. And then he would laugh like it was a joke.

• • •

Trying to teach Nile how to swim is like very patiently trying to teach a fish to walk.

In the best of circumstances, human bodies are just barely able to stay afloat. Compared to animals that belong in the water, we must look like chickens pathetically beating their wings at the air, attempting to take flight. But the slippery, squirming body of a five-year-old makes the feat nearly impossible. I've been taking Nile to pools on and off for months, trying to teach him, but we haven't gotten very far.

When we get in the pool, I make Nile look up at the ceiling and float on his back, keeping one hand underneath his head and the other under the small of his back as I guide him. He endures one pool length of this, but then he objects when I suggest that we practice holding our breath.

"No, Daddy," Nile says. "I want to swim."

"You have to learn to hold your breath if you want to learn to swim."

"No," Nile repeats. "I want to swim!"

He can sort of doggie paddle with a pool noodle stuffed under his arms, and this is how he spends most of his time in the pool in Boston, preferring to splash around and have fun, rather than doing the boring work of practicing and learning. I tend to let him do what he wants, because I want him to at least feel comfortable in the water, but I never let him out of arm's reach. Although he can hold his breath for a few seconds, he has absolutely no ability to get himself back to the surface if he goes under. Also, he takes more risks than he should, because, not wanting to scare him out of the pool,

I've never explained how a couple of lungfuls of water will *fucking kill you*.

Here, there are no pool noodles, but the shallow end is only three feet deep, and Nile is tall enough to touch. Smiling, he takes off for the deep end, marching off happily as the water rises to his neck, and then his chin, and then his mouth, at which point I have to scoop him up and drag him back to the shallow end, where he starts the whole process over again.

"I'm swimming!" he boasts as I haul him back to the shallows for the second time. "I'm having so much fun swimming!"

It feels like I should let him struggle for a second or two when he gets into trouble, to see whether he might be able to manage better than I think, or, at the very least, so that he can see that he's definitely *not* swimming yet and still has a lot of work to do. But I can't do it. There's always a moment, just a fraction of a second, when his head goes under the surface, and I can't tell whether he's holding his breath or if he's just another fraction of a second away from inhaling chlorinated water. I'm standing right there. Nothing bad is going to happen. But still, I see my son underwater, and my brain screams to *get him to the oxygen*, and so I do.

Forever, fathers have been teaching their kids to swim by tossing them into the water and watching as their survival instincts kick in. But the other thing fathers have been doing forever is *messing their kids up for life*. I'd be willing to bet that the events that have caused the bulk of the damage have been accompanied by the words, *This is the only way you'll learn.*

• • •

For lunch, we drive to a diner called the Flying Saucer, which is painted silver and built in the shape of two alien spaceships sitting side-by-side. The interior is all red and dark blue, and above our table hangs a poster depicting some Martians about to feast on a man, with the caption: *The fate of earthlings who do not pay their bill.*

It's nearly noon, and we've barely eaten anything yet. In the back of my head, I hear Belzie's voice telling me to feed Nile some vegetables with lunch, but he wants pancakes, and I'm not going to force him to choke down a side of broccoli with pancakes. Last night, at IHOP, I ordered a veggie omelet from the Simple & Fit menu, which made me feel grown-up and responsible. But today I'm starving, and I order the E.T. Special – buttermilk pancakes, sausage, bacon, ham, home fries, Texas toast, and three extra-large eggs – which makes me feel like a fat toddler with no self-control.

Waiting for the food, Nile quietly chants in the cadence of protest marchers: "Where … are … my … PANCAKES?!?!" and then, when I tell him to quit it, makes monster faces in the mirrored wall. When the food finally arrives, Nile wolfs down his pancakes faster than I can cut them up for him, and I easily clear the entire mountain of carbs and animal fat from my plate. On the way out, we get a strawberry milkshake and sit outside, sharing it with two straws. I'll start over on the no-sugar thing (or some other idealistic, unsustainable kick), when we get home.

On the ride back to the hotel, Alice calls, and I send it through the Black Racer's speakers so that Nile can hear her.

"Where are you guys?" Alice asks.

"Canada," I tell her. "We decided to stop off and see Niagara Falls."

"Canada!" Alice says. "I thought you were headed out this way."

I go through our itinerary with her again, explaining that we're seeing Belzie and Peanut in Chicago, and then continuing on to Waterloo without them. I've gone over this with her many times, as recently as yesterday, and she's only seventy-four years old, but in the past year, she's started getting confused more easily.

"How are you feeling?" I ask her.

"Oh, not too good." This is Alice's stock answer. Whenever we talk, she tells me how badly her rheumatoid arthritis is acting up, how she can barely use her hands, how she can't work in her yard the way she wants to. "I can't hardly get around anymore. But I need to get to the grocery store before my baby Nile comes out to see me."

She perks up as she says this last bit. I know she's been looking forward to our visit.

"Don't worry about us," I tell her. "Rest up, and we'll see you in a few days. I'll take you to the store when we get there."

"I'm overdue to go to the doctor," Alice says, her voice weary again. "But if it turns out that I have cancer, I'm not doing chemo or any of that. I'm just going to let it end."

Alice has been talking about dying ever since I can remember. When I was a teenager, she used to say that, when her arthritis got bad enough, she would go out to the garage and start up the car and just drift away. If she couldn't make it to the garage herself, she told me, I would have to help her.

"Cancer?" I say. "What, did you have a bad test result or something?"

"Oh, no," she says, casually, as though she's been talking about the weather. "I don't know, though. I haven't had a woman's appointment in ten years. Me and pap smears don't get along. When they've tried to give me one in the past, I've torn the wallpaper off the walls in two different doctor's offices."

I don't know the details of a pap smear, or whether ten

years is a long time to go without one. I don't know why they're still necessary for women who have had a hysterectomy, as Alice has. I certainly don't know what in the hell *wallpaper* has to do with anything. But I am eager to change the subject.

"We might be kind of tired when we get in the first day," I say. "Maybe we should push dinner with Grandma Wilson to the next night."

Alice and Grandma Wilson once hated each other, owing mostly to their longstanding disagreement about whether Alice stole Papa away from Grandma Wilson, or whether Papa and Grandma Wilson had already separated by the time Alice came along. But after Papa left Alice in much the same way he'd left Grandma Wilson, those bad feelings melted away, and the two of them even made a trip out to Boston together for Nile's second birthday party. Belzie jokingly wondered whether Papa, who was still alive at the time, might get excited by the idea of his two former lovers, now both in their seventies, sharing a futon in our apartment.

During the past two summers, Alice has traveled out to Boston by herself, and part of the reason we're taking this road trip is so that she can see Nile without us having to host her for a week. She has low expectations regarding food and entertainment, but she can still be a lot to handle. The first day or so is usually fine, but then she starts repeating herself, saying the same few catchphrases on a loop, like a toy with a pull-string: *Your cousin Wanda dresses just like a streetwalker! I don't hate anybody in the world, but I do hate your father! When I die, I don't want any fuss, I don't want any funeral – I don't want nothing!*

"Your Grandma Wilson wanted to know whether you'll bring Nile to her house," Alice tells me.

"I'd like to." I spent holidays in that house when I was

a kid, and I haven't been back for fifteen years. "But I don't want to go if my father is there."

"Well," Alice says. "He'll be there."

"Then I don't want to go."

"Oh God," Alice says, her voice dripping with contempt. "Isn't he just the pukiest person on earth?"

"He's pretty awful," I agree.

"I'm not awful!" Nile interjects from the back seat.

"Not you, baby." Normally, I would try to distract him here, to direct his attention away from these adult concerns. But I already broached the topic with him yesterday, and so I tell him the truth. "We're talking about my father. He's the awful one."

"He's worthless," Alice says. "Just as worthless as tits on a bull."

· · ·

Saturdays in Waterloo were Special Day. Papa and Alice would pick me up Friday nights and keep me through the weekend when I was four and five years old, and on Saturday mornings, we would go to a department store, where I was permitted to choose any "small-box" toy that I wanted – usually a He-Man action figure to add to my collection. I loved to crawl up onto Papa's lap while he watched television in his recliner, giving myself whisker burn as I nuzzled into his cheeks, breathing in the scent of his Brut aftershave and Old Spice deodorant. Alice found little excuses to give me money: a dime for wiping up a spill, fifteen cents for scratching her back, a quarter for saying she was my favorite grandmother. On nights when Papa was out, we would stay up late and watch re-runs of "Newhart" and "Night Court" until one of us got hungry, and then I would sit in the darkened kitchen and watch her make us grilled cheese sandwiches.

Eventually, Papa and Alice moved to the suburbs of Des Moines, and my mom and my brothers and I moved to Papa's childhood home in Maxwell, which he fixed up and rented to my mother for $250 a month. Although this put Papa and Alice in closer physical proximity to another set of my cousins, my brothers and I were still Alice's favorites, and so we were Papa's favorites, too. After we moved to Massachusetts, Papa and Alice would come out to visit us, and my brothers and I flew back to Iowa to spend several weeks with them each summer. On our first night back, Papa would empty out a huge jar of nickels, dimes, and quarters that he'd been saving up all year, and we would roll up the coins and take them to the bank the next day, each walking out with more than a hundred dollars in spending money for the summer. We rarely had to spend it, though. Papa and Alice took us to the mall to buy baseball cards and clothes and school supplies. Back in Massachusetts, we were still on food stamps and living in subsidized housing, but in Iowa, it felt like there was a limitless supply of money.

It also felt, as corny as this sounds, like there was a limitless supply of love. My father wasn't around, and although my mother loved us fiercely and did the best she could, she was overworked and overstressed and overtired, and my brothers and I never gave her a moment's peace. When she tried to talk on the phone with a friend or a bill collector, my brothers and I would fight loudly in the background while she held up an angry finger and frantically mouthed *stop it, stop it*. We would egg her on until she became red-faced and furiously hung up the phone, grabbing the worst offender by the hair and dragging him off to his room for a vicious spanking with a wooden spoon.

I would never call what my mother did "abuse." But if I

did those same things to Nile now, I would definitely call it that.

Papa and Alice had more time, more patience, more willingness to indulge my brothers' and my every childish whim. In their eyes, we were brilliant, hilarious, adorable. Everything we did was perfect.

And then I came back to live with them for good, and everything was different.

By then, the Des Moines bank had forced Papa into early retirement, and he was spending half of each year in Las Vegas doing handyman work, drawn by the warm weather, the income, and the opportunity to endlessly shove twenty-dollar bills into video poker machines. Alice stayed in Maxwell year-round, tending to the house and the yard. This didn't seem strange to me at the time. When you're a kid, you just accept the facts of your life as normal. But Alice was in her early fifties, and already she seemed to be running out the clock on life.

I thought that things in Maxwell would be the same as they were during the summers, when my brothers and I played in the enormous backyard all day and then dared each other to take ice-cold showers before curling up with bowls of ice cream in front of the television. But as the winter closed in on Alice and me, turning the skies black early in the afternoons and covering the ground in a crunchy layer of ice, something changed. Suddenly, I couldn't do anything right.

"Goddamn you," Alice would say through clenched teeth, if I so much as left a pair of socks on the floor, or forgot to use a coaster. "I'm not your nigger slave, here to pick up after you. You faggot."

I've tried not to think about these things for years, and now only a few details stand out. I remember how Alice would walk in on me changing clothes, and when I objected, she would say, "Oh, I don't want to see your deformed body." Once, she said she preferred Dolly Parton's version of "I Will Always Love You" to Whitney Houston's, and when I casually brought up the conversation the next week, Alice denied ever having said such a thing, screamed at me, and refused to make me dinner until I apologized for being a liar. She would dig her long fingernails into my wrists, clamping down until the nails nearly pierced my flesh. Once, when I pried her fingers off, she lost her balance and fell to the floor, then threatened to call the police on me for "abusing" her.

In front of my best friend, she rapped me on the knuckles with a thick plastic coat hanger. "Who in the hell do you think you are?" she said. "You're Calvin Hennick. You're nobody. You're nothing."

I was blindsided. I didn't know what had gone wrong, and I wanted to fix it. I made little vows to myself that I would be perfect, that I would stop talking back to Alice, that I would keep my room clean and always put my clothes in the hamper and never leave dishes around the house, and then she would start loving me again. But of course, I couldn't be perfect. If Alice was in the mood to find fault with me, it never took her long.

My mom told me I could come back to Massachusetts if I wanted, but I knew there wasn't room for me there, and I didn't want to admit defeat and go back to the place where I'd written the people off as snobby and cruel. If I couldn't make it in Massachusetts, and I couldn't make it in Iowa, either, then maybe Alice was right. Maybe I was the problem. When Papa came home during the summers, he would make a couple of meek attempts to stand up for me, but he didn't want to get in the middle of things, and when Alice started in on me, he would often just disappear.

Looking back as an adult now, I wonder whether Alice

was working through her own issues. Her mother died when she was four years old, and her father had been blinded in World War II, leaving her to look after her three younger brothers and sisters, even though she was a young girl herself. According to her own stories, she spent her thirties drinking and carrying on affairs with married men, but she sobered up after she met Papa. After she quit drinking, she started shopping, running up credit card bills that Papa ignored until they ran into the tens of thousands of dollars. When I was a teenager, she developed other little addictions, like the period of time when she ate nothing but Butterfingers. For a while, she developed a nervous habit of scratching at her arms with her long fingernails until she bled, and then she would spray the wounds with Aqua Net hairspray to clot them. The hairspray must have stung like all hell, but maybe that was the point.

If I have an armchair diagnosis, it's this: Alice had no control over her own life, and so she tried to control mine.

At the time, I wasn't interested in making excuses for her. I would stand in front of her as she berated me and try to take it, my eyes welling up as she searched for the combination of words that would tip me over the edge – *fruit faggot goddamn asshole loser just like your father*. No matter how hard I tried to contain them, the tears eventually spilled over, and then Alice would smile. "That's right, go ahead," she would say, mocking me as my face lit up with anger and shame. "Cry your fucking crocodile tears."

I wasn't perfect. Like every teenager in history, I thought I knew everything. If I could go back in time and watch myself, I'm sure I would be embarrassed by my own behavior, and there were no doubt plenty of times when Alice was right to be frustrated with me. I have no way of looking back objectively and seeing what was my fault and what was hers. I can only say how I felt at the time, and how I felt was so goddamn worthless and unloved.

I don't think I imagined that.

· · ·

Nile and I walk the half-mile from the hotel into Niagara Falls's touristy, kitschy heart. When we get to the city center, the first thing we see is a dinosaur-themed miniature golf course, which seems to be fairly new, with large and not-totally-unrealistic-looking dinosaurs guarding the putting greens. The gray flesh of the brontosaurus hangs in ripples off its flanks, and the gleaming white teeth of the T-rex appear to be razor-sharp. At the beast's feet, three vicious-looking little raptors struggle to claw out of half-hatched eggs. Just beyond the putt-putt course sits the massive Sky Wheel, and then Nile and I pass through a forest of laser tag arenas, ice cream shops, IHOPs, and wax museums. It's two in the afternoon, but many of the women already appear to be dressed to go out for the night, wearing colorful high heels and shimmery mini dresses. Eight-year-old boys on vacation with their families wear tee shirts with tough-guy slogans like "No Quit, All Commit."

Belzie and I came here together one April, before we had kids. The season was just beginning, and it felt like we had the entire town to ourselves, but today I have to hold Nile close to me as I guide him through a gauntlet of knees and elbows.

When Belzie and I visited, I had two years of sobriety under my belt, although I did suffer a small lapse during that trip. While wandering in and out of tourist shops, we stumbled upon one with a display case full of rolling papers and bongs and glass pipes. I spotted a little vial that cost thirty dollars, and asked the shop owner, a middle-aged Southeast

Asian man, about it. The owner told me that the vial was a tincture of salvia – a purportedly hallucinogenic substance that had, up to that point, largely been ignored by Canadian and American drug laws. I was curious, and I purchased the vial, putting some of the tincture under my tongue later that night when we got back to the hotel. I didn't experience any hallucinations, though, and so I tried a little bit more, and then a little bit more, until it was all gone, and then I insisted that we return to the store, where I demanded my money back.

"Look," the shop owner said, holding up a small mirror. "Look at your eyes. You're high."

"You're high!" I yelled, far too loudly. "You're the one that's high!" Belzie pulled me out of the shop, afraid I would get myself arrested.

When I'm not drinking, it's easy to forget how quickly it can take hold of me. I stayed sober for another year after that trip to Niagara Falls, but then, one night no different from the thousand sober nights that preceded it, I convinced myself I could drink just a little bit of whiskey. Before long, I was drinking by myself in my home office before noon on weekdays. I would quit, and then start again, and then quit, and then start again. The thing that worries me most about the alcohol is the way that it breathes life into the darkest part of me, the part that wants to sit and wallow, the part that wants to give up.

Nile and I walk toward the ticket booth for the Hornblower cruise, but we arrive to find two endless lines – one to buy tickets and another to actually get on the boat – and we decide that we'll come back first thing in the morning before leaving town. We snap a few selfies by the railing, with the American Falls in the background, but it's a struggle to get Nile to take a picture. When I do get him to look into the phone, his eyes and lips are so droopy with fatigue that it looks like we're having a miserable time.

We make our way back through the city center and duck into an arcade, where I buy twenty dollars in tokens. Nile has fun playing the driving games, pretending to pilot a wave runner, an ATV, a motorcycle, and three or four other vehicles. But when we try the games of skill, it turns out that we're spectacularly bad at winning prize tickets. We play a few rounds of skee ball and a game where we throw rubber balls at clowns' heads. At the end of each game, a lonely ticket pokes halfway out of the slot, and I have to bend down and yank on it to get the whole thing out. Meanwhile, the other fathers walk around with strips of hundreds of tickets draped over their shoulders, weighing them down like yellow pythons.

I try to teach Nile how to play air hockey, but right after I plunk four tokens into their slots and push in the metal tray to release the puck, he spots a NASCAR game behind me. It's not a racing game, or even a video game at all. It's just a thing where you roll rubber balls down an incline, and then a plastic stock car moves up a chute if your ball goes through the right hole. There isn't anybody else playing, and so it would just be us racing against ourselves. I can already guess what we would win: a single yellow ticket.

Nile is so enthralled by the prospect of this game, though, that he won't even attempt to play air hockey with me. "Nooo!" he says, setting down his paddle and starting toward the NASCAR game. "I want to play that."

"Get back over there," I say.

Reluctantly, Nile takes his spot at the table and places an indifferent hand on the paddle. He slumps his shoulders, pouting. "I want to play that."

"Hit the puck!" I find myself shouting over the din of the arcade. "Hit the puck!"

...

In the afternoon, we drive out to the go-kart track, and Nile tells me he tells me he wants to drive a go-kart all by himself.

"You're too small, baby," I tell him. "You have to share with me."

"But I drove the car by myself before."

"You mean at the arcade?"

"Yeah," Nile says. "At the arcade."

"That's different," I explain. "Here, you have to ride in a go-kart with Daddy."

We park in the gravel lot and get out of the car, and the air is filled with diesel fumes and the chainsaw sound of the go-karts. Then we round a corner and see the little cars buzzing around the tire-lined track, and I become strangely giddy. I'm a grown man with an *actual driver's license*. I have no business getting so excited about a go-kart ride. But I've been looking forward to this since Nile was two years old. I used to search online for car races and monster truck shows, but all the events seemed to start right around his bedtime, and I dreaded spending all that time and money only to end up carrying him out after a few minutes, kicking and screaming. He's growing up now. He's finally old enough to start doing all the things I've been imagining doing with him since he was born.

This part of Nile's life is only beginning, and yet, I can already feel it slipping away. At this moment, I'm Nile's best friend in the world. I only have a couple years of this, three at the absolute most, and then, although he will still love me, I'll slowly morph into his driver, shuttling him between the houses of boys his age who own violent video games I won't allow, and who listen to music by artists I'll have never heard of.

Nile finds a blue picnic table and sits down, watching as the go-karts race around the track. The Formula 1 style cars, with their brightly painted bodies, zip past first, trailed by the comparatively plodding black two-seaters.

"All right," I say after he's watched them circle the track a couple of times. "Let's go inside and get our tickets."

"I just want to watch," Nile says, his heavy-lidded eyes still fixed on the track.

"You can watch for another minute," I tell him. "Then it's our turn to ride."

"I don't want to ride," Nile says. "I'll just watch you."

"What do you mean?" I say, totally baffled. "You don't want to go?"

Nile nervously bounces his knee up and down. "We can't fit. I'll just watch you ride, because we can't both fit."

"No, see?" I point at one of the black two-seaters. "Look, there's a father and son right there."

"One person," Nile says, his voice a robotic monotone. "One person, one person, one person."

I'm not at all sure where this is coming from, but I'll be damned if we're not riding a go-kart. After booking the hotel for a second night, I'm several hundred dollars into this Niagara Falls side trip, and all we've done so far is eat at the spaceship diner and lose at skee ball.

"Come inside with me," I tell him. "Let's talk about it."

Nile grips my hand, and we enter the little building where the tickets are sold. I'm usually able to prod Nile into doing what I want without too much difficulty. I just have to figure out the right tactic. Sometimes he responds to reason, and sometimes simple reverse psychology works. Other times, I have to trot out the big guns: low-level guilting; old-fashioned bribery; or the nuclear option – *This is what big boys do, so I guess you'd better do it, too, if you want to be a big boy.*

"All we're going to do is watch them," Nile says. "I'm not driving with you! I'm not driving with you!"

"Calm down." I spot a picnic table at the back of the room and take Nile there, sitting next to him. "Talk to me instead of yelling at me. What's the matter?"

"It's because of the loud noise," Nile says, pressing his sharp little shoulder into my ribs. "And because the cars go really fast!"

"Oh!" I say, thinking that we've solved this. "The go-karts just look like they're going really fast, but they're actually slower than the Black Racer."

"They go fast," Nile says. "I can *see* them!"

"I can make it go slow," I offer. "Do you want me to make it go really slow? Come on, let's get our tickets."

Nile crosses his arms across his chest, keeping his gaze straight ahead. "I'm not going."

This is where I should drop it. It's just a go-kart ride, and Nile is scared, and he's only five years old, and this is obviously *not a big deal.* But something has been set off inside of me. It's not just that Nile has been begging to ride go-karts for more than half his life, and it's not just that my immature little man-feelings are hurt because my son is refusing to have fun with me in the specific way in which I demand that he have fun with me. It goes deeper than that. For some reason, it feels extremely important to me, completely out of all proportion, that Nile overcome this crippling fear. I know it's a small thing, but if Nile can't conquer his fear of a small thing, that feels to me like a big thing. I picture him climbing a diving board ladder as a teenager and then standing at the top, paralyzed by fear, before climbing back down. I picture him handing his lunch money over to a bully instead of standing up for himself. I picture him working up the nerve to ask someone to prom and then chickening out. If he can't get over his fear of a go-kart, it feels like he'll never get over his fear of any of these other little things, either, and if Nile can't work up the courage that it takes just to get through daily life, then I will have failed him as a father.

The stakes feel, to me, unreasonably high.

"I'm disappointed," I say, trying a new tack. "I want you to be brave, and I want you to try new things. I promise you'll be safe."

"I want to go home."

"We're going to sit here for a minute. We're going to sit here, and I'm going to be disappointed."

"We're going to the hotel," Nile says, spitting the words out in an authoritarian little bark. "Right now."

"Hey," I say, trying to regain control of the situation. "I'm your father. I'll decide what we do."

Nile grunts. "That makes me so angry!"

"Yeah, well," I say. "I'm angry, too."

This tips Nile over the edge. He begins full-on crying, loudly, here in this little room with only a half dozen other people milling about, buying their tickets and getting sodas from the vending machines. I rub my eyes and sigh into my hands.

"Waaaaaaaagh!" Nile wails, actually making that very sound – Waaaaaaaagh! – as though he's in a "Cathy" comic strip or something. "Eeeeeeeh!" he shouts. "Aaaaaaaaagh! Noooooo!" I think he's done, but then he catches his breath and screams, "Yaaaaagh! I'm not going on a go-kart."

"Fine," I say, unable to mask my totally inappropriate disgust. "Then I'm just going to sit here and be disappointed. I can't make you go on a go-kart if you don't want to, but I'm allowed to be disappointed."

"WAAAAAAAAAAAAAGGGGGGGHHHHHHHH!!!"

"Stop it, stop it!" I whisper-yell. People are staring. A

middle-aged Muslim woman wearing a headscarf looks at us almost quizzically, as though trying to figure out where this boy's mother is, and why anyone would leave this child in the care of a man so thoroughly ill-equipped to parent him. I can feel the judgment in her eyes, but I don't know whether she's judging me because I'm a controlling jerk who's torturing my child, or because I'm a softie who lets my kid throw tantrums in public. This is maybe the most central, essential question I have about fatherhood: Where is the line between these two extremes, and how do I walk it?

Normally, if Nile or Peanut are causing a scene in public, I take them outside, not wanting to disturb other people. But I'm not yet willing to admit defeat here. The obvious fact that whether or not we ride on go-karts is *not the end of the world* is, for the moment, only a faint scratching at the door of my mind. It barely registers over Nile's sobbing, or over the voice in my head that's screaming, *If you let him chicken out, he'll never be a man, and you'll be a shitty father*. My heels are dug in. I'm hoping, against the evidence in front of me, that Nile will somehow calm down and decide that I'm right, that go-karts are actually fun and not scary at all, and that we'll have a great time together if he just calms down and gets behind the wheel with me.

"Aaaaaaggghh!" Nile sobs. "Gaahhhh! Waaagghh!"

I take off my glasses and set them on the table and pinch the skin between my eyes. I take in a slow, deep breath through my nose. I rub my eyes with both palms until I see stars, and then I set my elbows on the table and rest my forehead in my hands. I stare down at the tabletop as it slowly emerges from the darkness. And, under my breath, I mutter, "You fucking baby."

Or, at least, I think it's under my breath. The words are so quiet that they don't even make their way to my own ears over the sound of Nile's wailing. But somehow, he hears me.

"YOU!!" he screams. Tears streak his cheeks, and slobber gushes from his mouth. "You said a bad word! You yelled at me!!"

I don't know what else to do, and so I stand up from the table and walk to the other side of the room, only five or six paces away, as though this will somehow allow me to escape the situation. If Belzie were here, I might take Peanut for a walk and leave Nile with his mother for a few minutes, and then we would all come back together and everything would be fine. But for now, Nile and I are stuck with each other.

"You!" Nile shouts again, pointing at me, his voice somehow growing even louder. "JUST YOU!!! It's all your fault!"

He's sobbing desperately. I press my fingers into my right temple, hard, trying to figure a way out of this. The woman in the headscarf looks at Nile, then looks at me; looks back at Nile, looks back at me. I have the sudden, nearly uncontrollable urge to explain myself to her, to make sure that she and everyone else knows that this isn't what it looks like. But of course, I worry that it's exactly what it looks like. I worry that I'm a terrible father with no clue what I'm doing.

I walk to Nile and put my hand his shoulder. "Come on, baby," I say. "Let's go home."

"He yelled at me!" Nile shouts, to no one in particular, still in the final throes of his tantrum. "He yelled at me!"

"Do you want to go back to the hotel?" I say. "Come on, let's go back to the hotel."

Nile smooshes his face into my ribs, streaking my shirt with snot and spittle. "I'm tired."

"I know you're tired," I say. "But I don't like how you're acting. And I don't like how I'm acting, either. So let's go to the hotel, and you can play with your sticker book. Do you need a hug? Stand up. Get a hug."

Nile stands, and I give him a squeeze, and he begins to calm down. Then I take his hand, and together we walk out of the little building and back to the Black Racer. I wish I could say that this is where I let things lie. The screaming and the crying and the swearing are all over, but even after he's strapped into his booster seat, I make a few last, futile stabs at browbeating and manipulating him. I tell Nile he'll regret not going on the go-karts later. I tell him he's making me sad. "I can make you a go-kart out of Legos when we get back to Boston," he offers, trying to find another way to make me happy. And finally, my brain fever breaks for a moment, and, like a big boy, I accept that I'm not going to get what I want.

. . .

On the drive back to the hotel, I notice for the first time all the signs for wine and beer shops lining the road. They're everywhere, and my eyes linger on each of them for just an instant too long. My brain dares my foot to hit the brakes.

I prefer whiskey to beer, primarily because it works more quickly, but it would be easy enough to find a liquor store and pop inside and buy a pint of Jim Beam. It would be easy enough to work my way through the bourbon in the hotel room, lying in bed with Nile beside me, watching television. No one would know.

It's not a real craving yet. It's just an idea, a suggestion at the edge of my mind. But I know from experience how little it takes for the tiniest thought to tip over into an uncontrollable urge. And here's the thing: The thought isn't totally irrational. Sure, if I start drinking again and keep at it, I know that I'll eventually ruin my health, and my career, and my relationships. I don't want Nile and Peanut to grow up with a drunk for a father. I don't want to push Belzie to the point where she has to seriously consider whether it's worth staying with me. But in the moment, there are real benefits to be had.

If I stop for whiskey, the pounding in my head will build as we make our way back to the hotel. The shame and anxiety will intensify, becoming nearly unbearable as I slip inside the bathroom, out of Nile's sight, and open up the bottle. But then, after I take that first drink, all the bad feelings will melt away, replaced by a warm bloom in my brain. I'm a squishy, nostalgic drunk. Some of the happiest moments of my life have been the times when I've stopped by the kids' rooms at the end of the night, pleasantly sloshed, and placed my hand gently on their backs, feeling the rise and fall of their breaths.

Nile is too young to know anything about booze. If I start drinking again and keep at it, he may one day look at me the same way I look at my own father now. But for today, all he'll know is that his daddy is cuddly and quiet and letting him watch cartoons. All he'll know is that his daddy has stopped hassling him about the stupid fucking go-karts. And every-thing will be happy, if only for this one moment.

Day 4

THE CITY IS GRAY and sleepy still as Nile and I make our way down to the river. The darkened windows of a nightclub reflect my bulging belly back at me, and the long stretch of parkland between the Space Needle knockoff and the Sky Wheel is strewn with last night's litter. Nile skips along the path while I plod behind him in my flip-flops. The only other person in sight is the driver of a golf cart-sized street sweeper, working to clean up a sprawling parking lot.

I would have preferred to let Nile sleep in, but I want to get us on the first boat to see the Falls, and then start out of town. Belzie called yesterday to tell me that our Chicago friends' newborn son has been hospitalized with a fever. He'll be fine, but our friends are no longer available for social outings, meaning that Belzie will now be alone in the city with a toddler in a sling. Before, I wasn't in any rush to get us to Chicago, but now I'm going to try to arrive right when Belzie does, around noon tomorrow. We'll make a little family vacation out of it.

But first we have to get on this fucking boat.

This is our third attempt. We tried again yesterday evening, after the drama of the go-karts, which by now is long forgotten. Instead of buying a pint of whiskey and hiding out in the hotel room, I brought Nile back to the river, and although the line for the boat was still a mile long, the sun was shining, and I bought us ice cream cones and finally took a decent picture of us with the white sheet of the American Falls in the background. In the photograph, Nile and I are looking at each other and laughing. It's a great picture, but by the time I saw it later on in the hotel room, I'd already forgotten what was so funny. Even though we have a photo of it, the moment is lost to memory.

As the afternoon turned to evening, we got in line to ride the Sky Wheel. I expected Nile to chicken out, but in fact, I was more frightened than he was, gripping my seat as we rounded the top of the nearly two-hundred-foot circle, warning him not to shake our gondola. Afterward, we played a round of dinosaur miniature golf, tapping our colorful golf balls between the monsters, feeling the heat on the backs of our necks each time the volcano at the center of the course shot out a plume of flames. By the time we grabbed a pizza, it was nearly ten o'clock, but the midsummer sun is stubborn this far north, and the sky didn't darken until we were back in our room. Nile sat at the window, looking out at the neon landscape, vigorously shaking his head as he ate. When I asked him what he was doing, he said, "It makes there be so many lights!"

"Oh, look!" Nile says now, as we round a corner and the Falls come into view. "Daddy, the waterfalls are smoking!"

"That's water vapor," I tell him. "The water is crashing onto the rocks so hard that it makes a mist in the air."

We buy our tickets and take our place in line for the boat, and it begins sprinkling rain. The line is much shorter than yesterday, but as it moves forward, it takes us through a hidden series of spirals and switchbacks, making it clear that there are unseen hundreds of people in front of us. While we're under cover of these ramps, the sky lets loose, pouring down rain like bullets. Nile hides his head under my shirt as the line creeps forward, burrowing into my belly. "I don't like it when strangers look at me!" he says.

Eventually, we reach the level of the river, where a teenage girl hands us flimsy red ponchos and then thrusts us back outside into the pelting rain. The ponchos are designed for the mist of the Falls, not for the deluge outside, and they succeed only in keeping our torsos dry. Our hair gets soaked immediately, and water drips down my glasses and drenches the bottoms of my shorts. The line keeps moving, but then, just as we get to the dock, the boat takes off, leaving us to wait in the rain for half an hour until it returns.

Nile only complains a little, and I try to entertain him. "I'm an apple," I say, puffing my poncho out around me as he laughs. "I'm a giant red apple!" I tell him I'm tired and ask him if there's a dry spot where I can sit down. "How about here?" I ask, pointing to a puddle, and he giggles and tells me no. "How about right here? Is this dry? No?!? What about here?" We pretend for a while that our ponchos are firemen's jackets, and that all this water falling from the sky is helping us to tamp down a blazing inferno.

The gray-haired man behind us has been watching us as we play, and finally he meets my eyes. "How old?" he asks, smiling.

"How old are you?" I ask Nile, but he bites his lower lip and turns away. I shake my head at the man in apology. "He's five."

The man nods to his own towheaded grandson standing beside him. "This one's eight." The boy smiles up at me, missing a tooth. "I haven't been here since my daughter was your son's age. Now, my daughter is your age, and her son is older than yours. The time just goes."

"Sure."

"Hold onto every moment," he says. "They grow up quick."

People are constantly telling you this when you have

young kids, that the time seems to pass in an instant. And while it's true, it's also a *super unhelpful* thing to say, because there's simply no way to put this information to good use. Before the trip, I was transferring some pictures from my laptop onto an external hard drive, and I looked through a few as I sorted through them. The moments are frozen in time, divorced from any sort of context. In one, I'm holding Nile inside a replica space capsule at the Museum of Science. I'm on my back, torquing my head around to look at the camera, and he's flailing around in my arms, but in the snapshot, we appear to be adrift in zero gravity. We look weightless. When I searched even further back, to when Nile was only a year or two old, the boy in the photos seemed like a stranger to me, so different from who he is now. Even though the memories are preserved in bits and pixels, I already feel like I've lost a part of him.

It feels pointless and impossible to try to hold onto everything. I think back to the hiccup in his baby laughter when I tickled his feet, but I can't quite remember the sound. I try to relive the memory of dropping him off at preschool, how he would go off to play with blocks, and just before I reached the door he would remember I was there and then turn and put his hand in the air to wave. And with the most vulnerable look on his face and the tenderest note in his voice, he'd say, "Bye, Daddy."

The door shuts. It's over.

The Hornblower boat finally returns to the dock and lets the other passengers off, and Nile and I file on board. The roof blocks the rain, but everybody is already soaked, and so no one bothers to take shelter, instead lining up along the rail to stake out the best spots for photographs. I buy Nile a hot chocolate, taking the lid off and blowing on it so he won't burn his tongue.

The boat pulls up first alongside the American Falls, and we watch as the boulders at the bottom turn the white water into a fog. I give my phone to a middle-aged woman to take our picture. Later, looking at the photos, I'll learn that she hasn't made even the slightest attempt at getting the gigantic waterfall behind us into the frame, but it doesn't matter. Nile is closing his eyes and burrowing into me, refusing to look at the camera.

As we make our way to the larger, more powerful Horseshoe Falls, the rain intensifies. The wind ripples our ponchos, and I put my phone away for fear of ruining it in the downpour. I try to look up to the top of the waterfall, nearly two hundred feet above our heads, but I can't see anything. The rain and the mist are blinding, and seem to have merged together, along with the gray of the sky, and the roar of the waterfall, and even with the boat itself, and with Nile and me. I feel outside of space and time. For a long, lingering moment, we're just electrons in a thundercloud. There's nothing to say, nothing to see, nothing to hear, nothing to do, nothing to think, nothing to worry about.

And then the boat turns around, and we're chugging our way back toward the dock.

. . .

Rather than crossing back over the border into New York, I decide to drive us through Canada, between the Great Lakes, and the enter U.S. again in Michigan. Samantha, the hotel desk clerk, tells me that the Detroit border is usually jammed, and so I aim instead for the Blue Water Bridge, up near the thumb of Michigan's mitten.

I'd assumed that this would be a Great American Road Trip through backroads in places like Pennsylvania and Ohio, but instead we're on the Canadian expressway, where exits are called "gates," and where there's a sign that I have to read three or four times before I can make any sense of it, which says, "Speed Measuring Warning Devices Prohibited."

The rain alternates between a gray drizzle and the sort of torrent that bombarded us in the morning, and at one point I spot a motorcyclist waiting out the deluge beneath an underpass. I'm more tired than I thought, and I keep yawning and shaking off the sleep that threatens to run me off the road. When we loaded up the Black Racer this morning, I noticed scratches on all four wheel rims, and now I'm nagged by the worry that I'll be charged for it. I know I didn't cause the damage. I haven't run up against a curb, or even parallel parked. But now that I've noticed the scratches, I won't be able to quit thinking about them. There's always something in my life causing this sort of low-level dread: a looming tax deadline, a suspicious mole. I really do walk around muttering "I hate myself," but it's always about tiny things that I forget about instantly. Later, I remember only the feeling, the sneaking suspicion that *there must be something the fuck the matter with me.* Occasionally, Belzie will overhear and ask me what I said, knocking me out of my trance and forcing me to sheepishly confess the monumentally stupid thing causing me to hate myself, like the memory of a time in college when I talked too long to a girl who was clearly trying to escape me at a party, or the time in high school when I didn't express sufficient gratitude for a gift given by a friend.

Do other people's brains turn on them like this?

After a couple hours on the road, we pull off for lunch, as much to get some caffeine in me as because we're hungry. Nile has been asking for Chinese, but all I'm seeing are the type of roadside travel plazas with four or five different fast-food options. At the place where we stop, there's a Tim

Horton's, a Wendy's, and something called New York Fries. I get Nile a hot dog and some water from New York Fries and set him up in a booth, then order a double cheeseburger with fries and a coffee for myself at Wendy's, plus a pair of small Frostys for the two of us.

I wolf down my food in a few bites, but Nile pokes fussily at his hot dog. He says he doesn't want the bun, and so I cut up the wiener for him, but then he claims he still doesn't like it.

"It's a hot dog," I say. "It tastes exactly like every other hot dog in the history of hot dogs."

Nile jabs at it with his fork and makes a face. "Well, it's not very usual."

"It cost me four dollars," I say, working my way now through my Frosty. "Eat."

Nile grumbles and stabs at a piece of the hot dog with his fork, then begins glacially nibbling away at the edges. It takes him nearly half an hour to finish the entire hot dog, and by the time he's moved on to his Frosty, the coffee and the double cheeseburger are fighting each other in my stomach, both desperately trying to escape.

"Let's hurry it up," I tell Nile. "I need to use the bathroom."

Nile takes two small bites of his Frosty and then pauses. "Brain freeze."

I try to wait for him to finish, but he keeps taking long, languid breaks, and finally I can't hold it anymore. "Come on." I grab his hand, and we get up and empty our trays into the garbage, saving a fistful of brown Wendy's napkins for Nile and his Frosty. "You're finishing that thing in the potty."

I hurry us into the bathroom, taking small, quick steps. At the far end, there's a handicap stall with a changing table inside, and I fold it down and set our atlas and the brown napkins on top. "Eat here," I tell Nile, not wanting him to drip his Frosty all over the floor. "Use it as a table."

And then I get my pants undone and sit down, and with my son eating ice cream not three feet away, I just completely devastate this poor toilet.

It's quite some time before I'm finally done, but Nile is still eating his Frosty, taking the tiniest bites and yet somehow still dripping all over the floor. I discover now that the bathroom isn't stocked with actual toilet paper, but instead has one of those dispensers that issues singe-serving sheets of one-ply that are both rough as sandpaper and thin as tissue. I pull a square out of the dispenser, and I can see my hand through it. Then I remember the brown napkins on the changing table, and I snatch them away from Nile.

He just stands there, finishing his Frosty, dripping ice cream down his fingers, as though none of this is happening.

I finish up, and we go to the sink to wash our hands. He's done with the Frosty, but he doesn't want to throw the cup away, because the garbage can is right next to the hand driers.

"What are you going to use?" he asks me, squirming nervously.

I finish washing and turn off the faucet. "What do you mean?"

"What are you going to use to dry your hands?"

"The hand drier," I say. "I'm going to use the hand drier to dry my hands."

"Oh!" Nile jumps from one leg to another. "Oh! Oh!"

I put my hands under the drier, which is jet-engine loud.

"Nooooo!" Nile shouts over the roar, covering his ears, his voice full of dramatic terror. "Not again!"

I take his empty Frosty cup from him and toss it in the trash, and then we walk out into the parking lot. Nile points across the lot to a man climbing up into the red cab of his truck. "See that man in the big rig?" Nile says. "Even though that man gets to drive a truck, is he going to have as much fun as we do?"

I smile to myself. The brainwashing is working. "No, baby," I say. "Nobody has as much fun as us."

• • •

The border crossing into Michigan takes more than an hour, but once we're back in the U.S., the road is wide open. As we pick up speed on the highway, I glance in the rearview mirror and see that it is filled with gray clouds. In front of us, it's all blue skies and sunshine.

We're not much closer to Maxwell than we are to Boston, and it's not as though the landscape has changed dramatically over the past few miles, but I immediately recognize where we are as the Midwest, and I feel a pang of homecoming. The highway seems suddenly more full of 18-wheelers and shit-kicker pickup trucks than it was just ten minutes ago.

Within a couple miles of the border, I spot a large, hand-painted sign. It's got a yellow background, and in large, red letters it just says: TRUMP. It looks like it was scrawled either by a child with a gigantic red crayon, or by an adult with a bucket of blood. At this point in the campaign, the consensus is that Trump will certainly lose Michigan, and that Iowa, a deeply purple state, will likely be a coin flip. He's trailed Clinton in national polls by mid-single-digits for most of the summer, and although he's clearly within striking distance of the presidency, the national media seem to still be deciding just how seriously to take his candidacy. Whether he wins feels almost beside the point to me, at least in terms of what his campaign has revealed about the country I love. I've already seen the way millions of people are gravitating to

Trump's old-school, no-apologies, bulldozing brand of masculinity. I've already seen the way people either thrill to or ignore the way he villainizes immigrants and minorities. I've followed politics my whole life, and Trump is the first major candidate whose rallies I would feel unsafe attending with my family.

I've been counting on the idea that the world will become a better place as my children get older, that the country will keep making progress. But watching the campaign, I worry that there's no such thing as an inevitable march forward. Maybe there's only a pendulum swinging back and forth.

We stop at the first gas station we see to refill the tank, and to let Nile use the restroom. The people at the station are all a little bit bigger than the people I would see pumping gas on the East Coast, and my schlubby clothes fit right in. One guy has a '90s goatee and double piercings in both ears, and he's wearing a heavy metal graphic tee shirt and camouflage cargo shorts. A middle-aged dad exits the store in khaki shorts, long white socks pushed down around his ankles, black rubber sandals, and an oversized tie-dye tee shirt that doesn't quite succeed in hiding the enormousness of his belly.

These are my people.

When we get back on the road, I set the cruise control to eighty miles per hour, which feels glorious after four days of suburban traffic and standstill border crossings, and Nile zones out while I fiddle with the radio. I find a station that plays all the country acts I listened to when I was in middle school: Shania Twain, Randy Travis, Hal Ketchum, Reba McEntire, Vince Gill, Sawyer Brown. I haven't heard, or even thought of, most of these songs for twenty years, but I find that I still know most of the choruses, and a few of the verses, too. The lyrics are intensely earnest.

If I die before I wake, feed Jake. He's a good dog.

She's in love with the boy! She's in love with the boy! She's in love with the boy!

Gotta thank Mama for the cookin', Daddy for the whoopin', the devil for the trouble that I get into. I gotta give credit where credit is due, I thank the bank for the money, thank God for you.

I stopped listening to country when I got to high school, switching to the grunge bands – Pearl Jam, Nirvana, Soundgarden – whose popularity had peaked a few years earlier. By the time I was fifteen, I looked down on anyone capable of enjoying music sung by a person wearing a cowboy hat. I remember feeling almost personally affronted when our class chose "Small Town" by John Cougar Mellencamp as our senior song, knowing I would have to walk out from my high school graduation to the lines, "Gonna die in this small town, and that's probably where they'll bury me." But now, these old songs make me homesick for all the things I miss about the Midwest. The room to roam, the laughably low cost of living. But most especially, the totally unironic, unembarrassed straightforwardness embodied by these country lyrics. *I'm happy! I'm sad! I love my dog!* There's no guile, no sense that the songwriters think they're smarter than their audience. It's just people telling stories.

. . .

I've been thinking about stopping for the night in Lansing, which is three hours from Chicago, but we're about to zoom by it, and Nile is still fast asleep. I need to wake him in the next half hour or so, or he'll never fall asleep tonight, but for now I'm happy to let him snooze. The cruise control is still set at eighty, and I'm remembering how relaxing driving can be when there's no traffic.

The radio station begins to crackle and fade, and I find a new one that plays even older songs, ones I've heard before but didn't grow up with. First up are The Judds, asking Grandpa to tell them about the good old days, when families prayed together and stayed together. I never understand this sort of blind nostalgia. The song came out in the eighties, meaning the "good old days" likely occurred sometime between when Hitler was gassing Jews and when blacks were getting their heads cracked open for sitting at lunch counters in the South. Next up is "All My Rowdy Friends Have Settled Down." I don't think I've ever listened to it all the way through, and I keep waiting for a mournful turn, where Hank Williams Jr. realizes he's trying to fill a void in his life with all this rowdiness. But no, in fact, the song appears to be an actual, honest-to-God lament that his friends don't want to get drunk and stoned anymore. When Holly Dunn comes on with "Daddy's Hands," a song about her late father's prayerful, calloused paws, I look down at my own hands on the steering wheel and try to imagine Nile and Peanut penning a tune about them after I'm dead: how soft and pink they were from years avoiding manual labor, how I was such an anxious wreck that I perpetually bit the nails down to the quick.

After a while, I see Nile's arms stretch up above his head in the rearview mirror and hear his little waking-up grunts and yawns.

"Oh," he groans, still stretching. "Ohhhhh!"

"You tired, baby?" I say.

"Yeah, I'm just a little bit tired," Nile says. "But I also feel good."

"You're a sweet boy," I say. "And you're a trouper. Do

you know what 'trouper' means?"

"What?"

"It means someone who doesn't complain," I tell him. "It means someone who can stay up late at night and drive a long time in the car and still have a good attitude."

I've only recently learned that it's *trouper* and not *trooper* – that the word means *tough like a ballerina or a member of a Broadway show*, rather than *tough like a soldier*, and now I laugh to myself every time I think of the word. I can't get over the fact that we have homophones meaning *theatre performers* and *trained killers*, and it's the theatre performers who have become synonymous with *people who tough things out*.

A bouquet of billboards for cheap motels sprouts up outside of Kalamazoo, and I take the exit, passing by a particularly rundown Motel 6 and driving on to a slightly less dumpy Quality Inn. Outside the entrance, a woman sits on a bench, talking loudly into her phone about a custody dispute. Inside, the desk clerk, who is missing both her top and bottom front teeth, is chatting with a man at the counter about the benefits of rolling your own cigarettes. I use my AAA card to get a 10 percent discount, and then Nile and I drag our bags down the Lysol-scented hallway to our room. We're a fifteen-minute drive from downtown, and I'm too tired to think about venturing out, and so I set Nile up with the television and order Chinese delivery from a place that gets four-star reviews online.

While we wait for the food, Nile watches a live-action show on Nickelodeon called "Nicky, Ricky, Dicky & Dawn," lying face-down at the foot of the bed, tilting his eyes up to see the capers of these insufferably preppy children. When the show ends, an old episode of "Full House" comes on. There's a scene where Danny hustles Joey at pool, and Nile cracks up along with the laugh track, even though there's no way he understands what's happening.

At home, Belzie and I aren't super strict about screen time, but Nile watches mostly research-based shows like "Blue's Clues" or "Daniel Tiger's Neighborhood" – stuff that, at least theoretically, won't cause much harm. When I was a kid, there weren't any restrictions on what I could watch. At seven years old, I decided that I didn't like my daycare center, and for some reason my mom agreed to let me stay at home all day by myself during the summer. I watched television from the minute she left in the morning until the minute she came home in the afternoon – starting with cartoons like "COPS" and "Attack of the Killer Tomatoes," then moving on to game shows and reruns of "Bewitched" and "I Love Lucy" during the middle of the day, and finishing up with trashy talk shows like "Donahue" and "Sally Jesse Raphael."

At night, I watched shows like "Married … With Children," and "Beverly Hills, 90210." It completely baffled me that some other kids weren't allowed to watch "The Simpsons." Once, when I was eight years old, my mom rented "Pretty Woman." She didn't mind me watching with her, but she quickly grew impatient with my questions. She had told me about sex the year before, and at the beginning of the movie, she explained that prostitutes had sex with people for money. But then, when a man drove by Julia Roberts during the first act of the film and shouted, "How about a freebie?" I asked my mom what that meant, and she snapped at me, "I told you, already! She's a prostitute!"

The Chinese food comes quickly, but it is an epic disappointment. Everything inside my Styrofoam box – the General Tso's chicken, the pork fried rice, the egg roll – has the same beige-gray tint that I associate with brain matter, and Nile's lo mein looks like somebody fried a 19-cent package of ramen noodles in oil and then mixed in whatever vegetative matter they could find at the bottom of their garbage disposal. My chicken is supposed to be crispy and spicy, but instead it's limp and doughy and as bland as mashed potatoes.

I can't figure out how the restaurant gets four stars, but then I see that our meals have come with a pair of dinner rolls, and I immediately understand. Any customer base that has, either explicitly or implicitly, demanded that they receive goddamned *dinner rolls* with their Chinese takeout cannot be trusted to credibly review a restaurant.

We eat sitting side by side at the large wooden desk next to the television, our food and our faces reflected back to us in the mirror that hangs on the wall. "Is your food yummy?" I ask Nile as he swirls up a bite of noodles on his white plastic fork.

"Um," Nile says. "Why does the broccoli look all gooey?"

I bite into a large fried triangle, which is apparently what passes for a crab rangoon in southwestern Michigan. "I don't know, baby."

"I don't like gooey broccoli."

"You don't have to eat it."

Nile pokes at his plate. "And why did they put gooey carrots in here, too?"

"Here." I push his lo mein to the side and scoop some of my fried rice onto his plate. "Eat this."

We each take another bite or two of our meals, but mostly we get by on the rice, and soon we've moved on to the fortune cookies. The place we order from in Boston doesn't do fortune cookies, and I realize that this is Nile's first time eating them. I still remember how magical they seemed to me when I was a kid, these cookies that could predict the future.

I tear open the plastic wrapping on one of the cookies and hand it to Nile, then open my own.

"Like this." I break my cookie into two pieces and pull

out the strip of paper. "*You will always have good luck.* That's what mine says. Now you open yours."

Nile splits his cookie in two and pulls out his fortune, and I lean over to read it for him. "*Everything will now come your way,*" I say. "That means good things will happen to you. Do you like that? Do you like your fortune?"

"Yes." Nile pops half the cookie into his mouth and crunches down on it. "It means nothing bad will ever happen to me."

"Well," I say. "It doesn't mean that, exactly."

"That's what it said!" Nile insists, his voice suddenly urgent. "That's what the cookie said, Daddy!"

"The fortune cookie doesn't know everything," I tell him. "Mine said that I will *always* have good luck. But sometimes I have bad luck. Remember how I got a flat tire one time? Was that good luck or bad luck?"

"Bad luck."

"Right."

"And I'm not perfect!" Nile says, still weirdly animated. "I don't have to be perfect! I try my hardest! Why does this fortune cookie think I'm perfect?!"

I put a hand on top of his head and run my fingers through his curls. "It's just a cookie, baby."

"Well, Mommy says that none of us have to be perfect," Nile says, his eyes wide. "You don't have to be perfect. And I don't have to be perfect. And everybody doesn't have to be perfect!"

"That's true," I say. "But you want to know something about me?"

"What?" Nile says.

"Sometimes, if I don't do everything perfect, or if I have bad luck, I get really sad."

It's a small admission, but it's another step toward opening myself up to him. I want Nile to see me as steady, as someone he can count on, not as an anxious, neurotic hothouse flower. But I also want him to know that it's okay if he feels this way sometimes. I want him to know that he's not alone.

"That's what happens to me, too," Nile says.

"What should I do instead of getting so sad?" I ask him.

I'm trying to create a little lesson for Nile, but I think that maybe I need the lesson just as badly as he does. I want to hold onto it, to remember it the next time I start muttering *I hate myself* over some tiny twenty-year-old mistake.

"Maybe you could just try again," Nile says, his voice both sweet and matter-of-fact. "And if I'm not perfect, maybe I could try again, too."

I look at him in the mirror. "So we're not perfect. But we're both going to try hard?"

"Yeah!" Nile says, energized by this new outlook. "We'll try hard not to be perfect!"

I laugh and give him a squeeze. "Okay, baby. We'll try hard not to be perfect."

Day 5

I WAKE UP UNRESTED, the bedside lamp shining in my eyes. I barely stayed awake during Nile's reading lesson last night, and although I'd planned to sleep in the other bed, I closed my eyes for just a moment after finishing his bedtime, and then I drifted off myself. Along with the lamp, I had to contend with Nile's fitful thrashing. I have a dim memory of briefly waking up and telling him to quit hitting me. Nile replied, still asleep, "If you keep stealing my lunchbox, I'm going to keep hitting you!"

Now, Nile is lying facedown and drooling onto his pillow, his butt pointed up in the air and his lips parted slightly, like two little flower petals. I pull the sheet up over his body and get out of bed. There's sediment inside the coffee maker, and I wipe it down with a washcloth and make myself a cup. The coffee isn't good, but I try to drink it anyway, sitting up and reading in the other double bed, waiting for Nile to wake up.

He sleeps for two more hours, until 9:30. The trip must be pushing him to his limits. But when he finally gets up, he tosses off the covers and hops out of bed, happy and full of energy.

"Hey, buddy," I say, handing him a box of chocolate milk. "We're going to see Mommy and Peanut today. Drink this, and then we need to take a shower."

"Maybe later," Nile says, twisting away from me. "I want to play with my stickers."

"No, you have to take one now." Neither of us has

showered yet during the whole trip, not counting getting drenched in the rain at Niagara Falls. "I don't want Mommy to think I turned you into a piggy."

Nile giggles. "I'm not a piggy!"

I sniff at the air. "Mommy's going to smell you and say, 'What did Daddy do with Nile? Why did he bring me this piggy?'"

"I'm not a pig!" Nile declares, letting out a belly laugh.

"All right, then let's get in the shower."

In addition to hand driers, and go-karts, and the prospect of the kindergarten lunchroom, Nile is scared of showers. This one, I actually understand. Showering is a skill. You need to know how to let the water fall down your face so that you can still breathe, how to blink your eyes at the right time, how to adjust the water so that it's comfortably warm but not scalding. When I was Nile's age, showering was a bit like what I imagine waterboarding must be like, but with the added torture of shampoo burning my eyeballs.

Nile strips down while I adjust the water temperature, and then we step into the tub together. I fill up a little plastic cup with water and give it to Nile to pour over himself, then let the warm water wet my hair. When I open my eyes, Nile is holding the cup under my penis.

"What are you doing?" I ask him.

"You're dripping water," Nile says. "I want to get more water."

"Stop that." I snatch the cup away and fill it under the showerhead for him.

Back at home, Nile takes baths, and it's strange to be standing naked next to him like this, washing our potbellies together. Other than his stomach, Nile's body is all bones and taut little muscles. The top of his head already rises higher than my bellybutton. I'm certain he'll be taller than me, and I wonder how old he'll be when he surpasses my height.

Nile washes himself for a while, and then I take a turn with the washcloth, trying to scrub all the sweat and the sunscreen from his skin. Belzie has sent a special conditioner for his hair. I'm not certain whether I'm supposed to leave it in or rinse it out, and so I try to split the difference, doing a sort of half-assed job of washing it out of his hair.

Nile gets out of the shower before I do. While I finish up, he wipes the fog off the mirror with a hand towel and dances naked, unembarrassed, watching the wiggle of his own reflection.

• • •

I bang the baggage trolley through the hotel's front doors and get the car loaded up. Nile has just learned how to undo his seatbelt, and when I buckle him in, I make him promise that he won't unbuckle it until I give him permission. Only a few days ago, I read a story about a kid who died in a car accident, and his mother told the newspaper that he was always taking off his seatbelt, no matter how much she protested. I feel like I would try pretty hard to keep Nile from unbuckling his seatbelt while we were driving down the highway. But all it takes is one moment of not being perfect, and your kid is dead.

I steer the Black Racer back onto the interstate, pointing out a cornfield irrigation apparatus to Nile. "You're going to start seeing a lot of cornfields in this part of the country," I tell him. "Soybean fields, too. And we'll probably start smelling some pig poop."

"Pig poop?" Nile says. "Ewwwww!"

"It's not so bad," I tell him.

Belzie makes fun of me because I think that manure has a

sweetish smell, the same way that overripe fruit or even sun-baked garbage can smell a little sweet. But more than that, it reminds me of home.

Along the highway, one farmer has erected a billboard on his land. The sign has Jesus's face on it, next to the mystifying words, "The Supreme Court writes about abortion, but God writes about the murder!" Next, we pass a series of medical advertisements. "The Genius of 3D Mammography is Here!" declares one sign. Another, for a vasectomy clinic, says, "No scalpel! Get one side done, the other side is free!"

Belzie and I are done having kids, and although it would be kind and responsible for me to get a vasectomy, the truth is I'm just a coward when it comes to letting people near my scrotum with scissors. Belzie got an IUD implanted just a few days ago, and today is the last day she's under strict orders from her doctor "not to put anything in the vagina." That global phrasing – that "anything" – just slays me, as though there's really some danger of her putting literally "anything" up there: desk lamps, cantaloupes, cell phone chargers. *No, Belzie, get your car keys out of there! Don't you remember what the doctor said?!?!*

I see an advertisement for swimming pools, and suddenly I remember Nile's and my swimsuits, still hanging on the back of the bathroom door at the Niagara Falls hotel. I tell Nile this, and he gets upset until I assure him that we can buy another swimsuit somewhere between here and Iowa, where my friend Brice's sister has an above-ground pool. "We might not find a swim shirt, though," I tell him. "You'll just have to wear sunscreen."

"But then everyone will see my belly button," Nile says. "That's a private part!"

"It's not really a private part," I tell him. "You don't want anyone touching it, but it's okay if people see it."

Nile is unconvinced. "I need to hide it!"

"Okay," I tell him.

"I don't want anybody to see my belly button!" he says.

"We'll figure it out."

"Hey," Nile says. "What are belly buttons for, anyway?"

I tell him about how there was a tube that helped to feed him when he was inside his mommy's tummy, and how he didn't need the tube anymore after he was born, because now he could drink milk.

"Where was I before I was in Mommy's tummy?" Nile asks.

"Nowhere, baby," I tell him. "You weren't anywhere."

This seems to confuse him, and he's silent for a minute. Then, he asks, "What did I look like right after I was born?"

"You were crying," I tell him. "Your face and your body were red, and you were crying. And I cried, too, because I was so happy."

"Did you cry like a baby?" Nile asks. "Like, 'Waaggh!! Waaggh!'?"

"No, not like a baby. They were quiet tears. Happy tears."

Belzie and I still hate the hospital where she gave birth. A nurse talked her into an epidural she didn't want, and then an anesthesiologist stabbed her in the spine with a needle for over an hour, messing it up repeatedly while they made me wait outside the room. Her doctor missed the birth. The monitoring equipment lost track of Nile's heartbeat, and they almost wheeled Belzie into surgery before an 80-year-old doctor we'd never met threaded a scalp monitor inside of Belzie and onto Nile's head, leaving a bump that took weeks to go away. And then the epidural wore off right as Belzie was pushing, and she screamed and screamed.

But when Nile came out, red-faced and wailing, I became, in that instant, more human. More connected to the rest of the universe. As a teenager, I attended youth rallies in mega-churches, and I would stand with the other kids, listening to Christian rock, holding my hands up to the ceiling, trying to feel the power of the Holy Spirit. But instead of transcendent, I felt empty. As an adult, I've tried to meditate, but I can't even quiet my mind, let alone reach some higher plane of consciousness. Having kids, I believe, is the closest I'll ever come to reaching some next level, something truly beyond myself. Not something I'm *trying* to feel, but something that's just there. Undeniable, indescribable. It's not supernatural. It's the most natural thing there is.

Having kids is the first part of the actual, factual, biological Meaning of Life: to make more of ourselves, and then get the fuck off the stage.

"Did you touch me after I was born?" Nile asks.

"I did touch you," I tell him. "Your skin was so soft and buttery that it felt like it would slide off your bones."

"And was I slippery?"

I try to remember. "You were a little bit slippery. But the nurses dried you off, and then they put you right on top of Mommy's chest, and you drank milk from her boobies."

"Her breasts," Nile corrects.

"Yes," I say. "Her breasts. And then we brought you home. I'd never had a baby before, so I was scared, and – "

"Happy," Nile cuts me off. "You were happy."

"I was happy, but I was scared, too," I tell him. "I wanted to make sure you were okay, and I didn't want to do anything to hurt you."

Having him in our apartment that first night was the strangest thing. Neither of our mothers offered to stay with us. Or maybe they offered and we waved them off, thinking we could handle things ourselves. But either way, Belzie and I were alone with this tiny person who barely seemed to know how to breathe. The nurses and the doctors were all gone, and there was no one coming by to check his vitals every few minutes, no one to press gently on his belly and say things like, "He's a keeper!" Belzie was exhausted enough that she slept that first night, but Nile kept making little phlegmy, gaggy noises, and I was terrified that he would suffocate himself.

"The first night you were home," I tell him, "I was scared, and I brought you to the living room and watched TV all night while you slept on my chest."

"What show was it?" Nile asks.

"I don't know what show it was."

"Was it a show about cars?"

"I didn't care about the show," I tell him. "All I cared about was that you were healthy. And I've loved you every single day since then."

"You love me every single day?" Nile says.

I say it again. I'll never stop saying it. "I've loved you every single day since then."

· · ·

It's toll, traffic, toll, toll, traffic, toll, and then we're finally in Chicago, running an hour later than I'd hoped. Belzie and Peanut are already at the condo that Belzie booked through Airbnb, in a neighborhood called Wicker Park. I steer the Black Racer down a main drag populated by cool little hipster bars and tapas restaurants and tattoo parlors, and then turn we off onto the pretty, tree-lined street where the condo is located.

The rental takes up the second floor of a two-story brownstone, set back from the street behind an iron gate. I have to hit the call button a few times, but finally Belzie buzzes us in and meets us at the top of the stairs. We've woken her from a nap, and she's groggy but pretty, wearing a flowing paisley dress and Birkenstocks, her thin braids all twisted together into one big meta-braided ponytail. At first I think she's randomly wearing one blue sock with her sandals, but this turns out to be an ankle brace she's purchased from CVS.

"Hey," Belzie says, squinting at us.

Nile rushes past me up the stairs and squeezes Belzie around the waist, and then I haul my suitcase up over the last step and give her a peck on the cheek. It's a habit that's spilled over from the winters, when someone is always sick, and we avoid touching lips for fear of spreading germs.

"Is Peanut asleep?" I ask her.

Belzie nods toward one of the bedrooms, where the white noise of an iPad app is hushing and shushing. The condo is clean and modern, with polished hardwood floors. A bay window in the living room looks out onto the street below, and a television hangs from the exposed brick above the fireplace. There's a square glass dining table, and a faux white orchid sits in the center of it.

Belzie sets Nile up with a TV show, and then she and I sit at the table for a while, showing each other pictures and swapping stories. I tell her about Nile playing with the other kids outside the Hall of Fame, and she tells me about how patient and grown-up Peanut acted when the TSA agents at Logan insisted on checking the inside of her arm sling for explosives.

I met Belzie in New York when we were both 22, during our summer training for Teach For America. I'd come to the city with big plans to date every woman in New York, but my monogamous nature quickly won out, and Belzie was living with me by the next April. Personality-wise, she's a cat: reserved and plotting and standoffish; whereas I'm a dog: bound by the current moment, quick to trust, in need of constant attention and affection. I've asked Belzie many times what attracted her to me in those early days, and she's only ever been able to give me trivial details, silly things like the fact that I wore my shirtsleeves rolled up. For my part, I can't say exactly why Belzie stood out above everybody else. She's beautiful and smart and hardworking, but I met lots of women in New York who were all of those things, and I didn't think of marrying any of them. Belzie and I just fit.

Part of what drew us together, I think, is that we both felt like the poor kids in a city bursting with wealth and glamour. We had more resources than the students we taught, sure, but not nearly the money or the pedigree of most of our peers. I made a joke during the summer training about how I was the poor kid from a state school who didn't know how to tie a Windsor knot. Another corps member, who'd attended Georgetown, looked me dead in the eye and said, with no hint of irony, "You don't know how to tie a Windsor knot?"

Belzie and I married when we were 25 years old. Skittish from my family's dismal track record in this arena, I cornered everyone I came across in the weeks leading up to the ceremony, asking either how they'd made their marriage work, or, if they were divorced, what had gone wrong. I got sitcom-cliché advice about keeping my mouth shut and letting my wife buy as many shoes as she wanted. I got some better advice about how a marriage can't succeed if each person is putting in 50 percent of the relationship's effort, but only if both are putting forth 100 percent of their own effort. I'd always thought my Uncle Jim had divorced his first wife because she didn't want kids, but when I asked him, he told me, "I knew when she was walking down the aisle that it was a bad idea."

Belzie tells me that we occasionally get stares from strangers, but I almost never notice them. When we'd been married for two years, we took a road trip through the South, and although we were disturbed by the Confederate monument outside the Alabama statehouse dedicated to the "knightliest of the knightly race," people were largely friendly to us during our dozens of stops at barbecue joints and antique shops and Waffle Houses. Then, on our way home, we stopped for gas outside Blacksburg, Virginia. I pumped while Belzie hunted for snacks in the store, and when I went inside to pay, I got a strange vibe from the woman behind the counter. On our way back to the car, I said to Belzie, "That cashier was a racist, right?" Yes, Belzie answered. When she'd first walked into the store, the woman had looked her up and down and said, "Do you know where you *are,* honey?"

I don't foresee anything like that happening when I bring Nile with me to Iowa. He's five. The world may one day make his blackness a problem for him. But it hasn't started yet.

. . .

From the bedroom, I hear a whimpering, barely perceptible over the white noise of the iPad. I bolt from my chair and rush down the hall, knowing that Belzie will try to beat me there if I don't hurry. When I open the door, the whoosh of the white noise gets louder, and I see Peanut, still on her stomach in the middle of the queen bed, rubbing at her eyes with her non-sling hand. Seeing me, she tries to sit up, but she can't quite get upright with only one good arm. I pick her up out of the bed and squeeze her into my chest. I kiss her head, and she pulls her face back from me and looks at me with her big Cindy Lou Who eyes and says, "Da-Da!"

"Oh my God." I give her another kiss on her forehead and breathe in the smell of sleep and shampoo. "I love you so much."

I try to carry Peanut out of the room, but she wants to walk by herself, and so I set her on the floor. She toddles down the hallway, her three little afro poofs bouncing lightly, and meets Nile for a hug. She's half his size, but Nile is gentle with her, wrapping his arms loosely around her back and resting his cheek against her head. At home, they bicker, swiping each other's toys and crayons, but they really do love each other. If anything, Peanut bosses Nile around. A few weeks ago, she told him to go sit in a timeout at the bottom of the stairs, and he actually obeyed her.

Belzie fishes a pack of fruit snacks out of her bag, and I pick Peanut up and sit at the table with her in my lap and try to feed her. But she squirms down, out of my arms, then begs to be picked up again, then squirms once more. She wants to both be in my lap and down on the floor with Nile, and she's upset that she can't do both at the same time.

"I want fruit snack!" Peanut says.

"Here." I rip the bag open. "Daddy gives them to you."

"No!" she squeals.

"You want Daddy to help you?"

She glares at me with toddler-meanness. "Noooo!"

"Oh," I say. "You want to scream at me?"

"Yes," Peanut whimpers, and then presses her head gently into my neck.

• • •

Nile and I bonded instantly. His favorite place to be was on my chest, and he would nap there, his sweaty head leaving a wet spot on my shirt just above my heart. During his first year, I stayed home with him in the day while I finished my final year of graduate school, teaching and taking classes at night. I was the only dad at the mommy-and-me playgroups.

Peanut, though, didn't much like me for the first eighteen months of her life. She was more interested in food than affection, and after nursing with Belzie, she would often fuss until she was put back in her bassinet. She wasn't interested in cuddling with me. I was busier, too, done now with grad school and working full-time. Peanut stayed at home with a nanny while I worked in my office upstairs during her first year, and often it seemed like she loved the nanny more than she loved me.

After she started daycare, I would rush downstairs from my office when Belzie brought the kids home in the afternoons, but Peanut would shriek when I tried to give her a hug, turning to her mother to save her. I believe that it's important to let children, especially girls, decide when and how they want to be touched, and so I didn't force her to cuddle me. I would just give Nile a hug and then slink back up to my office to finish my work.

Then, Peanut got sick. It happened slowly, over the course of months, and it came on so gradually that Belzie and I didn't even notice. There was a bloody stool, but her pediatrician said it was nothing. A few months later, she wasn't eating much, but we thought she was just being picky. Then she had trouble sleeping, and we chalked it up to a botched sleep-training attempt. Finally, we took her to the doctor again. The pediatrician who saw her this time ordered a full blood work-up, and then called us that afternoon and told us to head to the emergency room. Peanut was deathly anemic.

Children's Hospital admitted her and gave her a blood transfusion, and Belzie stayed overnight with her while I went home with Nile. The next morning, the very first test they ran came up positive. Something called Meckel's diverticulum, a rare intestinal defect. The problem had been causing her to bleed out through her poop, so slowly that we didn't even notice the blood. They scheduled surgery for that afternoon.

This was all very routine for the doctors. They performed the surgery with a scope, rather than cutting her open. And there were, of course, hundreds of kids in the hospital in far worse shape than Peanut. But Belzie and I were terrified, and we were angry with ourselves for not seeing earlier just how sick she was. We were still getting to know her. To us, it seemed like she was just a small, fussy, wan baby. We didn't know she was dying right in front of us.

The recovery was worse than the surgery. The doctors gave her morphine, but it suppressed her breathing, and she briefly turned blue. After that, she only got Tylenol and ibuprofen to help her deal with the pain. They put her on IV fluids, but she wasn't allowed to eat or drink anything until her bowels "woke up" again, and it was awful to watch her get even skinnier as she starved in her tiny hospital bed, connected to half a dozen wires, with a tube shoved up her nose and down her throat to suction the green bile out of her stomach. Most of the time, she was too weak to complain, but occasionally she would whimper and cry, saying simply, "Away! Away!"

Belzie mostly refused to leave Peanut's side during her nine days in the hospital, but I convinced her a couple of times to go home and take a shower. It was during one of these times that I was alone with Peanut that she finally pooped. She was lying on my chest in her diaper and her hospital gown, resting her sick little face on my shoulder. And then she let out a grunt and made a poop, and I started sobbing with relief – big, ugly, uncontrollable sobs. Aside from the kids' births, this bowel movement was the absolute happiest moment of my life. It was the first time I knew for sure that Peanut would be okay.

She warmed up to me after that. She became less dependent

on Belzie, more receptive to the games that I'd played with Nile when he was the same age: Baby Bomb, where I pick her up horizontally and lift her up to the ceiling, then drop her down onto the couch, catching her again at the last instant; Go Horsey, where I put her up on my shoulders and snort and buck and gallop, pretending to try to shake her off as she laughs.

She lets me tickle the spot under her chin. She cuddles up with me to read, and she runs up to me and squeezes me around the legs when she comes home at the end of the day.

Other times, I'll ask Peanut if she wants a hug, and she'll say, "Daddy, I busy!" or else reject me with a casual, chirpy, "No!"

And that's fine. We have plenty of time.

• • •

The train station is half a mile from the condo, which should be a ten-minute walk through pretty side streets, but Nile and Peanut both seem determined to delay us as much as possible. Nile, I think, is a combination of tired, emotionally overwhelmed from seeing Belzie and Peanut again, and a little jealous that he's not getting 100 percent of my attention anymore. And Peanut is just a toddler.

Belzie wears the black Ergo baby carrier over her colorful dress, but Peanut wants to be with me, and I carry her in front of my body, straining my back. Belzie is supposed to have Nile, but she gives him a wider berth than I would, letting him walk down by the sidewalk by himself, and he's hiding behind trees and running across driveways without looking.

"Nile!" I shout, seeing him approach another driveway.

Belzie finally takes his hand, but Nile hangs on her arm, putting all of his weight onto it and shuffling his feet along the sidewalk instead of walking. "Can you stop?" Belzie says. "Just walk like a normal person."

"Nile not a person!" Peanut chirps.

"Nile's not a person?" I repeat, delighting in the silly turn of phrase.

But Nile gets angry and pouty. "I am a person!"

Belzie tries to joke with him. "Peanut was confused," she says. "She thought you were an ape."

"No, Peanut!" Nile shouts, genuinely horrified. "I'm not an ape!"

"Nile ape," Peanut says.

Carrying her is getting to be too much, but Belzie won't give me the Ergo, concerned that I'll mess up the length of the straps. I try handing Peanut off to Belzie, but Peanut swipes at Belzie's face and screeches as Belzie tries to force her into the carrier, only calming down when Belzie sets her on the ground and lets her toddle along by herself. So now we're all doomed to travel at a baby's pace.

We make it to the train station, eventually. We buy some 24-hour passes, then climb the stairs to the elevated platform. Belzie wants me to take her picture with the kids next to the tracks, but I refuse until she takes two big steps back. She's more protective of the kids when it comes to small things like winter coats and sunscreen, but I'm far more cautious when it comes to big things like hurtling trains.

"No subway train has ever jumped off the tracks!" Belzie protests.

I lower my phone, signaling my stubbornness. "You know how I am."

Belzie moves back, and I snap some photos.

"Chugga chugga choo choo!" Peanut says. "That's a train sound."

"That's not the sound of a subway train," Nile informs

her. "That's a steam train sound."

Peanut retorts with baby talk. "Goo goo ga ga."

After twenty minutes underground, we emerge again into the sunny city, hustling along crosswalks between skyscrapers on our way to Grant Park. I remember coming to Chicago for the first time during college, for a journalism job fair where absolutely no one was hiring, not even for internships. I walked through the streets wearing a suit I'd purchased with my own money at J.C. Penney, and looked up at the gleaming skyscrapers wondering, *Who lives here? Who works there? How did they get here? How do I?*

We stop by Cloud Gate and Crown Fountain, then duck into a little garden outside the Art Institute and get ice cream cones for the kids. Nile finishes his quickly, and soon there is much whining and wheedling about why we can't *just go already* and how he is *tired of sitting here* and how he doesn't *want to wait anymore* and how he's *going to leave now.* I try to get him to come and sit next to me and calm down, and Belzie says that I'm babying him, and I say that I don't want him wandering off into the street. And she says that the garden is enclosed, and I say that it is definitely not enclosed, that the street is *right fucking there*, and Nile keeps saying how he just wants *to leave* and this *isn't fair.*

I can feel the fatigue from the trip beginning to wear me down, and I'm letting Nile's behavior get to me more than I should. When we're alone together, I'm typically more patient with him. But now that we've reunited with Belzie, a part of me wants to let her be the adult, to plug my ears and yell *shut up shut up* while she handles things.

Peanut finishes her ice cream, and we move on to Maggie Daley Park, which is home to the most fantastic playgrounds I've ever seen. They're separated by age level, spread out over a series of small hills and valleys, surrounded by the mirrored skyscrapers that ring the park. Belzie takes Peanut to a baby swing, and I follow Nile to a huge play structure that looks like it's been plucked from the imagination of a little boy, all drawbridges and turrets and twisting, four-story slides. From the top, flags and windmills and weathervanes poke up randomly, as though scrawled in place by a child.

"This bridge is wobbly!" Nile shouts, forgetting his moodiness. "Let's go up here! I think I can do it myself. Wait, no. Can you help me?"

I give Nile a boost up a little ladder, and then he's lost in a dark maze of rungs and stairs inside the bowels of one of the turrets. My heart stops for a beat when he leaves my sight. It's a big city, and Nile doesn't even know my phone number, and what if he gets lost, and what if he falls, and *what if and what if and what if*.

The kids play for nearly an hour, as the slowly setting sun flirts with the tops of the skyscrapers. When I catch fleeting glimpses of Nile, he's smiling and laughing with the other kids. But when it's time to leave for dinner, he melts down.

"Just a *few* more minutes?" he pleads, his voice near a sob.

"Oh," I say. "That's how big boys act. They whine."

Nile stiffens his spine and calms his voice. "Um, maybe just five more minutes?"

"Sorry, buddy," I say. "We have to go now."

Suddenly, his voice is desperate again, and a little bit mean. "Maybe just one more minute!"

"Belz?" I say.

Belzie looks up from rummaging through her bag for hand sanitizer. "What?"

"I've been doing this for four days straight," I say. "Could you maybe – "

"Just two more minutes!" Nile shouts. "Just two more

minutes!"

Belzie takes him by the hand, and I carry Peanut, and for a moment we're able to distract Nile with promises of a special, unusual kind of pizza. But when the play structure recedes behind us – when he understands that we're really leaving and not coming back – Nile dissolves into a full-fledged, ALL-CAPS tantrum. "NOOOOO!" he screams. "NOOOOO!!!"

It's not the words that cause me to bristle, or even the volume, but the urgency in his voice. It's the same manic, pleading caterwauling he makes when he's in actual pain. The same sound he made when he was two years old and stepped on a shard of glass, and the ER doctors made me hold him down while they tried to get it out with tweezers. It's a sound that makes me feel like I'll go insane if I don't escape it.

Rationally, I know this isn't a big deal. Kids throw tantrums; that's what they do. Getting upset about it is like visiting Seattle and complaining about the rain. And yet, I can feel my shoulders tense, and a faint but persistent urge to kick something. Not Nile, but something.

Nile stops screaming for a moment, but his breath is still staggered and frantic. "But I wanted –"

"Stop," I cut him off. "You're having a fun day in Chicago with your family. If you're going to talk to me about being sad, I don't want to hear it."

Nick sticks his lips out in a pout. "I'm not talking to you anymore."

"That's completely fine," I tell him.

With that, he's screaming again. I pick up my pace, leaving Nile with Belzie, still carrying Peanut in my arms. "Goddammit," I say, shaking my head.

Peanut smiles up at me and says, "Mammit!"

• • •

Everything is better at dinner. We've called our pizza order in ahead at Giordano's, but the pie still arrives more than an hour after we do. While we wait, we get the kids a plate of spaghetti and butter, and the food immediately calms Nile down. When the pizza comes out, it's a lake of bright red tomato sauce, held in by doughy walls of crust. Belzie and I stuff ourselves, and still we have to bring half the pie back to the condo with us.

"I'm glad I'm wearing a maxi dress," Belzie says, although her waist is as trim as the day we married. "Otherwise, my belly would be bulging out against my pants."

"Maybe that's the secret," I say, patting my own stomach. "Maybe I need to start wearing maxi dresses."

It's dark by the time we leave, and late for the kids to be out, and we sit in a food coma as the train rumbles back to Wicker Park. Because of the noise of the train, and my general state of half-consciousness, I am only vaguely aware at first that there is a crazy person screaming at the other end of the train car. I lived in New York for two years, and I am used to this, people yelling about Jesus coming back, or about how the government is corrupt. But gradually, the man's words come into focus, and I look toward his end of the car, seeing him for the first time. He's a white guy in his late twenties, slightly pudgy and decked out in Bulls gear, his eyes alive with hatred. He's not just ranting into the void, I realize now. He's threatening to rape the woman sitting across from him.

"I'll fuck you right in the ass, you stupid fucking bitch," he says. "You don't have no face, no ass, no nothing. I'm gonna come to your house, bitch. I'm gonna fuck you up. You fucking dick-breath, bitch-ass slut."

The reason I didn't register this earlier, I realize, is because everyone else on the train is pretending it isn't happening. The woman, a plain brunette around my age, is sitting with her boyfriend, and they're both looking off into the distance, trying not to make eye contact with the ranter. Everyone else is acting as though this is just a garden-variety lunatic, and not someone who's threatening to hurt this specific woman. Even her boyfriend doesn't interject with a "Hey, man ..." or simply take her arm and walk away.

My first instinct is to stand up and put my body between the lunatic and the woman. I'm not a tough guy; I'm not going to get into a fight. But I want to at least show this woman that the people on the train aren't going to sit by and watch as this man tears her limbs from her body. Belzie and Peanut are a few seats down from us in the other direction, though, and if I get into the middle of this, I'm either going to have to leave Nile by himself or else drag him along with me.

And so I do nothing, just like everybody else.

• • •

After we put the kids to bed back at the condo, Belzie and I sit up together for a while at the glass dining table in the living room. She drinks a cup of tea, and I make my way through the last of a two-liter of Diet Pepsi. At home, we rarely have moments alone like this. Usually, we wait until Nile and Peanut are asleep to eat, foraging separately through the fridge and pantry for something we can scarf down while we finish up work before bed.

Even though Belzie was only a few seats down from us, she didn't see the man from the train, and I describe the situation to her now – the crazed look in the man's eyes, the scared look in the woman's.

"I've been talking to Nile on the drive out here," I tell her. "I'm trying to figure out what I think about what it means to be a good man, and to tell him those things as clearly as I can. I told him is it's important not just to respect women, but to protect them if they need it. Not that I want him to have some sort of savior complex. But tonight, I felt like it was the responsibility of the men on that train to make sure that woman felt safe. And I was a little scandalized that nobody did anything."

"Maybe." Belzie sips from her tea. She's wearing a navy dress with pewter buttons, her black-rimmed glasses, and dangly fake-gold earrings. "But sometimes the best way to handle a nutcase like that is not to respond at all. You're not going to disarm that guy with words. You're only going to escalate things, and then instead of shouting, you have fists flying, and then the woman gets punched in the face instead of getting yelled at."

This is typical of the two of us. I'm more likely to jump headlong into a situation and think about the consequences later. Belzie is more thoughtful, more cautious.

"What else have you told Nile?" she asks.

I mentally rewind through the trip. "We talked about race a little bit, about Jackie Robinson and segregation. But I didn't go any deeper than that. Stuff like implicit bias, white privilege, de facto segregation – I don't think he's old enough to understand all that."

"He's not," Belzie agrees. "But this is just the beginning of these conversations. His understanding will keep evolving as he gets older."

"It's hard for me to know how much of this is going to affect him," I say. "Maybe we'll make progress fast enough that none of this will matter as much in ten or twenty years. Or maybe he'll be light enough that people won't even read him as black."

"No," Belzie says. "You're being naive. Even if he's the light-skinned guy hanging out with four of his black friends, they're all going to get the same shit. It's going to matter."

I'm silent for a moment. It's impossible for either of us to know what the future will look like for our children, but Belzie obviously knows more than I do about what it means to be black in America right now. Overt incidents pop up only occasionally. When she first moved here, she worked as a cashier at a supermarket, and an elderly white woman asked for the manager to scan her groceries instead, because she didn't like black people touching her food. When she's alone with the kids, people sometimes mistake her for the nanny. She's had the N-word yelled at her in traffic. Once, she bought a wagon from someone on Craigslist, and when she went to pick it up, the guy kept bizarrely insisting that she must live in the housing project down the street. But even day-to-day, she's told me, Belzie feels a pressure to be "perfect," to keep attention off herself. She makes sure to keep her hands visible when she's walking through stores. She makes sure not to talk too loudly at restaurants. Black men have a whole different set of experiences, experiences that neither Belzie or I will be able to speak to Nile about first-hand.

"I've talked to Nile about more basic things, too," I say, changing the subject. "I've told him that good men take care of their families. That they work hard, that they treat people with respect. And then, for myself, I've been thinking about stickier questions, like how much I should protect him from adversity, and how much I should let him make his own mistakes. What do you think? Is it too much? Am I overthinking things?"

Belzie pauses, thinking out her answer. "It's not that it's too much," she says, finally. "These things are important. But is this really what this trip is about for you? Lunatics on trains? Jackie Robinson? I feel like you have more personal things to deal with."

I raise an eyebrow. "What's more personal than figuring out how to raise my son?"

"Your family," Belzie says. "Your dad."

"My dad?" I roll my eyes, just slightly. "I've been telling Nile about all that stuff already. I'm an open book. I'll talk to anybody about it. I've only waited with Nile because of how young he is."

"There's a difference between talking about it," Belzie says, "and dealing with it."

I pour myself the last of the soda, keeping my eyes on the glass. "Sometimes I forget that my dad even exists. And when I do think about him, it's not like I get angry about everything all over again. At this point, I just feel numb."

"Maybe that's the problem," Belzie says. "You might feel numb on the surface, but this stuff is going to affect you in other ways if you don't deal with it."

She doesn't spell out what she means, but she doesn't have to. She means my constant anxiety. My occasional depression. My on-again, off-again drinking.

"What do you want me to do about it?" I say, sounding more defensive than I'd like. "I can't just walk around being angry all the time."

"You're driving to Iowa," Belzie says. "Have you thought about going to see him?"

"No," I say, as evenly as I can manage. "No, I haven't."

Belzie pushes out her chair and begins to remove her earrings, getting ready for bed. "Maybe you should."

Day 6

PEANUT IS IN BED between Belzie and me when I wake up, rowing herself around the sheets with her non-sling hand, yelling, "Noooo! Noooo!" in a high-pitched whine.

"What's wrong?" I manage, my eyes open only a slit. "Come get a hug."

"Nooo, Daddy!" Peanut screeches. "I want to watch a mooo-vie!"

"A movie?" I mumble. Through the haze of half-sleep, I see that Belzie is still deep in slumber.

"Nooo!" Peanut says. "Not a movie!"

I try to calm her with a pat on the back. "Not a movie," I say. "That's right. Not a movie."

"Noooo, Daddy!" Peanut says, increasing her volume, offended that I keep getting this wrong somehow. "Want to watch a movie."

I jab Belzie in the shoulder with my index finger. "What the hell is she talking about?"

Belzie turns toward the wall. "Just take her out of the room. You've slept all night, and I've been up with her."

I rub the sleep out of my eyes. "She was up during the night?"

"A movie, Daddy," Peanut whimpers, letting out a pathetic little sob at the end of her demand. "Want to watch a movie."

I take her to the living room and lie across the couch, and she sits on top of me like I'm a bench. When I click on the TV,

"Dora the Explorer" is playing, and Peanut quiets down and watches the show. I love this feeling, holding her while I'm still only half awake. "I love you," I whisper.

"Aya-yoo too," Peanut replies.

A commercial comes on for something called "Gemmies." It's some sort of jewelry-making kit, and while it looks fun and creative, I'm startled by the way the seven-year-old girls in the ad look like grown-ups. There's nothing inappropriate about what they're wearing; they just look like miniature adults, the way they have their hair and makeup done. One of the reasons that Nile and Peanut don't watch commercial television at home is that we don't want to let professional marketers tell them, *This is what it means to be a girl, this is what it means to be a boy.* Peanut is more interested in dolls than Nile was, but she also loves trucks and dinosaurs and super heroes, and I don't want her watching anything that will make her feel bad about not wearing lip gloss or having shiny yellow hair. Yesterday at the airport, Belzie told me, a woman complimented Peanut's "mile-long legs." Belzie didn't know what to say. "They're baby legs," she told me, recounting the story. "She has baby legs."

It doesn't take Peanut long to miss Belzie, and after a few minutes, she leaves the couch and the glow of the television and toddles her way down to the bedroom. I follow her, trying to coax her back to the TV so that Belzie can sleep for a few extra minutes, but Peanut ignores me. She goes to the side of the bed and starts petting Belzie's face. "Mommy," she says.

Belzie pulls the covers up around her head. "Why, Peanut? Let me sleep. You and I aren't the same person!"

"Mommy," Peanut says, yanking on Belzie's arm. "Mommy, Mommy, Mommy."

Belzie sighs, swings her legs over the side of the bed, and

stands up. "The feeling," she says, "is not mutual."

Nile wakes up a few minutes later, his sheets soaked with pee. I can't remember him ever wetting the bed before, not even when we first started potty training. He must be exhausted. There's an in-unit washer and drier, and the mattress is protected by a waterproof cover, so I just strip the bed and throw everything into the washing machine. As I'm doing this, I see Peanut crouching next to the coffee table in the living room, grunting like an Olympic weightlifter while she shits in her diaper.

I blink, trying to think of what it was like to travel before we had kids, before we had to plan our itineraries around little people's naps and bowel movements. I can't quite remember.

· · ·

We make our way to the train, stopping for glazed donuts and coffee. We eat at the counter at Stan's Donuts, and Nile keeps asking why we can't get on one of the buses that parade endlessly outside the shop window. He's always begging us to take him on public transit back in Boston, even though it's almost always faster and easier for us to drive, and sometimes Belzie will take him on a bus or a train just for the "fun" of it. I get a pen and a sheet of paper and draw him a crude map, explaining the concept of a bus route, and how we have to get on the right one, or else we'll end up in the wrong place.

After we take the train downtown, we wait at a stop for nearly twenty minutes for our bus to the Peggy Notebaert Nature Museum in Lincoln Park. It probably would have been faster just to take the Black Racer, but I'm happy to leave the car parked for the day, and Nile is more than happy to be taking the bus. As we sit waiting, he points to every non-bus vehicle and says, in a robotic monotone, "Not a bus.

Not a bus."

At the museum, the kids chase butterflies in a greenhouse, busily dam up rivers at water tables, and learn about ecosystems from a spinning wheel that Nile calls a "time machine." Peanut wears her silver dollar-sized admission sticker smack in the middle of her forehead, and she squeals in protest every time I try to remove it for her.

For Nile and Peanut, a couple of days in Chicago barely registers as a vacation. Their childhood is so different from my own – the way they beg to go to Indian restaurants, the way they're accumulating passport stamps while they're still in preschool. I never left the country until I was twenty-four, a jaunt to Montreal with Belzie during our spring break from our teaching jobs, followed by a ten-day trip to Peru and Bolivia that summer. Belzie and I are still both incredibly cheap, irrationally fearing that our middle-class existence will one day up and leave us, but travel is one of the few things we're willing to spend money on. We fly coach, and we stay in modest hotels, and we don't splurge on fancy dinners out. But we go.

The four of us wander through an exhibit about scientific specimens, and Belzie points to a human skeleton, showing Nile where Peanut broke her clavicle. She's relating the science to something in his life, which is good teaching, but still, I raise an eyebrow. Nile has been asking questions about death for weeks, and I know that this skeleton is going to turn into a *thing*.

"I can't believe somebody took all that person's skin off!" Nile says.

"Well," Belzie says, working her way into a sentence she clearly has no idea how to finish, "it's more likely that somebody ... died. And when you die, all your skin and muscles melt away, and what's left is a skeleton."

"Oh," I deadpan. "This is going to go well."

Nile has a look of horror on his face. "I don't want to be a skeleton!"

"You're not going to be a skeleton," Belzie says. "You know why?"

"Why?"

"You're healthy, and you're young, and you're not going to die soon." Nile just looks at her, and Belzie puts her hand up. "High five!"

Nile does not give her a high five. "Yeah," he says. "I'm healthy, so I won't die. And you guys won't die, either, right?"

Belzie hesitates, searching for a way to say *no of course I'll never die* while somehow not lying to him. She's saved by a taxidermied deer, which catches Nile's eye from its faux woodland habitat.

"I'm a monkey," Nile announces, bouncing onto the walkway through the life-sized diorama, surrounding himself with dead animals that stare out at him with glass eyes.

I follow him into the exhibit. "That's more of a forest than a jungle."

"I'm a crocodile!" Nile says. "Chomp! Chomp!"

. . .

Around a year ago, a bird flew into our kitchen window, bounced off the glass onto our deck, and died.

It traumatized Nile, who had never heard of death before. He even refuses to believe that the meat he eats is really dead animals, referring to "chicken the food" and "chicken the bird" as though they're two entirely different things. And although I've tried to gently disabuse him of this misconception, I honestly haven't tried all that hard, partly because I'd rather not talk to him about death any more than I have to at this point, but also because I need him to shut up and eat his goddamn food once in a while.

"Fix it, Mommy," Nile said, pointing at the dead bird. "Fix it, Daddy." We told him there was nothing we could do. "But what about the bird's mom and dad? They're going to be sad!"

Since then, Nile has been bringing up death randomly, more and more as time goes by, trying both to understand it and to reassure himself. One morning, on the way to pre-school, he claimed that I'd said he would never die. "I never said that," I told him. "Everything that lives dies. It's a sad thing, but it shouldn't be scary. And usually, it happens when people or animals get very old and their bodies stop working. You're not going to be old for a very long time."

Nile, it turns out, is as selfish as I am. You always hear about little kids freaking out that their parents might die, but it didn't even occur to me to be worried about that when I was a kid, and Nile doesn't seem all that concerned about it, either. We're both just looking out for ourselves. Except, of course, that I now have Nile and Peanut to worry about, and the idea of them dying is *way* worse than the idea of me dying. The decision to have children, to expose yourself to that sort of vulnerability, is almost literally insane. That vulnerability makes you more human in a way, but it also makes you kind of a terrible person. If I had to choose between Nile dying and every other five-year-old boy in Massachusetts dying, it would be tough fucking luck for all of those other incoming kindergarteners. The selflessness of parenthood creates its own sort of selfishness, because really it's not selflessness at all, but rather a sort of doubling down and reordering of self-interest, so that it now includes not just yourself, but your children, too.

So far, Nile isn't buying the death-is-sad-but-not-scary

thing, because of course he isn't, because who really does? It's a nice sentiment, the sort of thing that allows us to convince ourselves that we'll be able to face the end without whimpering, but it's pretty obviously bullshit. We're all terrified, even if we believe that there's nothing – or: Nothing – to fear. Most of life is just distracting ourselves from the fact that we're going to die, and we're really good at it. I'll go weeks or months without ever pausing and remembering and really knowing and even briefly trying to face the fact that the world will one day go on without me. I'm not even sure I really believe it. I'm not sure any of us do. Because if we really thought we were going to die one day, how could we possibly waste time on bullshit like traffic and mediocre television shows and – God help us – reading through pages of hateful Internet comments when we really ought to go to sleep? The only way we can do any of this shit is to pretend that it's going to go on forever.

The only difference between children and the rest of us is that children don't pretend that they're not pretending. Adults can find ways to ignore the hard, obvious facts of the matter until we forget about them, but Nile has to literally pretend – has to say the words "But I'm not going to die!" and truly believe them – in order to fool himself. And when I tell him, "No, sweetheart, one day your body is going to stop working and stop moving, and then you'll be dead," he doesn't do the grown-up version of pretending. He doesn't come up with a list of reasons about why that's okay, or talk about how death is just a part of life, or say that it's sad but not scary. Instead, he just says the most obvious, truest, most heartbreaking thing. "I don't want to die."

Papa died three years ago, and his ashes are buried in the Maxwell cemetery. I haven't been back since he died, and I'm planning to visit his grave when we get to town. I'm not sure how Nile will handle it.

I've only ever lied to Nile about death once. A few weeks before the trip, Belzie was at a meeting one evening, and I was serving up dinner for Nile and Peanut at the kitchen table. Nile mentioned how Peanut couldn't do something or other, because she was only a toddler, and I said, "Yeah, that's right, but one day she'll be as big as you. And then one day she'll be as big as me!"

"I'll be as big as you one day, too," Nile said, and already I knew exactly where this shit was going. "But I won't die, right?"

So, I went into my whole routine about how everybody dies, but usually it doesn't happen until people get very old, and then their bodies stop working. And he said to me – just listen to this – he said to me, "But Daddy, if my body stops working, won't you take care of me?"

And I stopped. My breath stopped. My heart stopped. At that moment, for just that moment, my own body quite literally did stop working. And then I went to him, and I held his head, and I lied to him. "Yes, baby," I said. "I'll take care of you."

. . .

After the museum, we try to take the kids out for lunch, but the Mexican place I find on my phone turns out not to be a Mexican place at all. In actuality, it's something called "contemporary," which, judging from the menu, seems to be a cuisine composed entirely of omelets and quiches. This won't work for the kids, who are starting to display the early signs of a hunger-induced meltdown, and so we feed them 7/11 hot dogs at a pocket park and then take an Uber back to the condo.

Belzie puts Peanut down for a nap while I do a reading lesson with Nile, and then I set him up with a TV show and reheat last night's deep dish leftovers in the oven. After fifteen minutes, I hear the hush of the white noise app grow briefly louder and then fade again as Belzie emerges from the bedroom. She comes and sits across from me at the glass dining table, but we're too tired to talk, and we both stare at our phone screens as I wolf down the deep dish.

The pizza is even better than it was last night, somehow. The crust is still fresh, the flavors have had more time to mix with one another, and the cheese is only slightly less liquid than fondue. It's mid-afternoon, and I haven't eaten anything since my morning donut. I can't get the pizza down fast enough. And then I feel a long string of cheese make its way down my throat and get stuck there.

I panic. I start working the muscles in my throat, trying to gag the cheese back up, but it won't budge. In the span of a second, I look at my phone and think of dialing 911, then look at Belzie and wonder whether she'll be able to perform the Heimlich, and then look at the empty chair next to me and consider performing the maneuver on myself, which I read about once.

It's only now that I realize that I can still breathe through my nose. The cheese isn't in my windpipe. But I still can't cough it up, and also can't swallow it, and I worry that it will make its way to a place where it will obstruct my airway. Finally, after what feels like forever but must only be a few seconds, I gag the gooey cheese back up into my mouth and spit it out into my napkin. It's likely that I was never in real danger, but still, I'm shaken.

Belzie, this entire time, has not once looked up from her phone.

I gasp dramatically. "Um, did you happen to notice that I

was choking to death over here?"

"Mmmm," Belzie says, not lifting her eyes.

"What the hell?" I say.

Finally, Belzie looks up at me, blinking. "What?"

"I was choking!" I say, anger already beginning to displace my fear. "What's so important that you can't even be bothered to look up from your phone when I tell you I'm choking?"

I want her to say she's sorry. I want her to put her phone down and come over to me and put her hand on my shoulder and ask me if I'm all right. But I can tell from the steely look in her eyes that this isn't going to happen. I can tell that she feels like I'm attacking her. And when Belzie feels attacked, she doesn't give an inch.

"I don't appreciate you coming at me like this," Belzie says, no note of emotion in her voice. "I didn't do anything to you. You're tired. Go lie down."

"I'm not tired!" I say, although this is clearly untrue. "I was choking! And I was scared. And it's fine if you weren't paying attention. But why can't you just say you're sorry instead of arguing with me about it?"

"I told you I was sorry already," Belzie says.

"No, you didn't!" I say. "You didn't apologize. Why do you do this? Why can't you just say you're sorry, and that you love me, and that you hope I don't choke to death?"

"I didn't do anything to you," Belzie repeats. "Take a nap."

This is how it always goes. The more animated I get, the more Belzie shuts down. She sees my agitation as an attack against her, and I see her flinty affect as a deliberate unwillingness to give me the basic love and reassurance that I need. When we get into one of these spirals, the only thing to do is to take a break and cool off until we've both forgotten about the dumb thing we were fighting about. But in the moment, I can't see what we're doing. I can only see that I'm asking my wife to love me, and that the answer is something other than yes.

"Just be nice to me," I plead. "Why can't you just be nice to me? If you asked me to be nice to you, my answer wouldn't be, 'Go lie down, you need a nap.'"

Nile appears at the edges of my vision. He's up off the couch and wandering into the orbit of our fight. "Mommy *is* nice," he says. "Daddy, Mommy *is* nice."

"Nile," Belzie says.

"Everything is fine, buddy," I tell him. "Go watch TV."

"But Mommy *is* nice," Nile says again.

"Yes, Mommy is nice," I agree. "Now go on, go back to the couch."

Nile returns to his show, and Belzie goes back to her phone. I stare at her as she sits there, looking down, scrolling through text messages, and with every second I can feel the pressure in my head building. I know that I'm losing all perspective of the situation, but I can't help it. What I want – a warm word, a kind touch – is so simple that it feels like Belzie would only withhold it if she hated me.

"Seriously?" I say, finally. "You're seriously going to just sit there and not talk to me?"

Belzie looks up at me, exasperated. "What do you want from me?" she says. "I'm sorry, okay? I'm a cold, awful person. Okay?"

For a moment, I consider packing Nile's and my things and driving to Iowa a day early. That's how angry I am. But instead, I take Belzie's advice and go lie down. Peanut is napping in our bed, and so I go to Nile's room, bringing my laptop and trying to read the news, but my eyes won't focus on the words. I can't think straight. I can't even articulate why

I'm so upset, and because of this I begin to suspect that I'm the one at fault here. But this feels almost beside the point. The thought that keeps running through my mind is so baby-ish that I'd be humiliated to repeat it to anybody: *Why won't she be nice to me? I just want her to be nice to me.*

My mind is spinning. It's a sunny summer afternoon, but I feel darkness descending on me. For the second time in just a few days, I feel the urge to drink gestating somewhere inside of me. I'm desperate to change how I feel.

Some minutes pass, and I flit from one site to another on my computer, reading the first couple sentences of a million different news stories, comprehending nothing. I feel trapped inside my own head. And then Nile comes into the room. He lingers at the door for a moment, seemingly unsure of how to negotiate the terrain of his two fighting parents.

"Nile," I say quietly. "Come here, buddy. I have some-thing to show you."

"Um, what is it?" Nile says. "What do you need to show me?"

"The biggest hug ever," I say.

Nile climbs onto the foot of the bed, and I shut my laptop and set it to the side. Then he flops onto my chest, and I pull him tightly into me. His bony knees dig into the sides of my ribcage, and his soft cheek rests against my shoulder.

Almost instantly, I feel the pressure inside my head begin to go away, like air being let out of an overinflated tire. Squeezing Nile into my chest, I feel the same release of ten-sion that I experience when I swallow down a large gulp of bourbon. It's an incredible relief, but it also makes me feel ashamed. This is not the father I want to be. I should be com-forting Nile, not the other way around. If I'm the sort of man who needs his own son to save him, then I'll never raise Nile into the sort of man who can take care of himself.

I know what needs to happen next, and I squeeze my eyes shut tight, dreading it. If I'm being honest with myself, I know what's happening here. I know where this constant need for love and affection and validation must come from, and I know this thing will eventually pull me under if I let it. Belzie is right. I need to deal with my family shit.

I've been trying to make this trip into an intellectual adventure, a grand exploration of masculinity and fatherhood. And it is that. But, I realize now, it has to be something more. Holding Nile in my arms, it becomes clear to me that I'll only succeed as a father to the extent that I'm able make peace with my past. And I'm about to drive right towards it.

I've avoided tackling this stuff head-on for a long time. During my longest stretch of sobriety, three years in my late twenties, I saw a therapist, an ancient, white-bearded man who ran his practice out of his home. When we talked about my family, he asked me how it all made me feel, and I said, "What do you mean?" It hadn't occurred to me that I was allowed to feel anything. The facts of my life were just facts. It felt silly and pointless to apply words like "sad" and "angry" and "disappointed" to them – words lifted from a kindergarten-classroom chart of emotions, so simple they could be represented by yellow circles with frowny faces and squiggly lines and inverted eyebrows drawn onto them.

I didn't want to be dramatic, I told the therapist. I knew that plenty of people had worse lives than I did, and I didn't want to spend mine boo-hooing my mean grandmother, my weak grandpa, and my worthless father. I didn't want to walk around feeling sorry for myself.

"What's the line from Mercutio, right after he's stabbed, just before he dies?" the therapist mused. Then he paraphrased from memory. "'The wound isn't so deep as a well, or wide as a church door, but it's enough.'"

He looked at me in silence for a long moment, waiting for me to take in his meaning. "Your family problems may not be the worst problems anyone has ever handled," he said, finally. "But that doesn't mean they're not important. Just look at how they're affecting you. They're enough."

Day 7

"I WANT MY MOMMY!" Nile sobs as we walk out of the Chicago condo and into the crisp morning.

I gently palm his head and guide him toward the Black Racer. "I want her too, baby. We'll see her again in a few days. I'm sorry you're sad."

"I want my mommy," Nile repeats, his voice full of fatigue as much as sadness. "I don't want to say goodbye."

He's been whining since the moment he woke up and saw me packing our bags. It's grating, but I sympathize. Maybe Nile really does need his mommy. Maybe we've had all the fun we're going to have, and I should just let him get on the plane back to Boston with Belzie and Peanut, and head on to Iowa alone to deal with the things I need to deal with. But it's too late now. Even if this trip ends up being a mistake, we're committed to it.

An hour passes in the car, and as the urban landscape of Chicago gives way to the Great Plains, Nile's whimpers fade away, and he turns his attention toward what's in front of us and away from what we've left behind. The freeway morphs into a two-lane highway as we speed toward DeKalb, the road's shoulders littered with old tire rubber, its ditches banked by endless fields of six-foot-tall corn. The country station on the radio advertises a police-sponsored fishing event called "Cops and Bobbers." A yellow sign on the side of the highway warns of "Loose Cattle."

We enter a miles-long construction zone. Nile perks up a

bit, sitting up higher in his seat to see the men in orange vests operate their front loaders and skid steers. Already, though, he's not quite as obsessed with trucks as he used to be. When he was two and three years old, he would shout and point out the window every time he saw a work vehicle. It got to the point where Belzie and I would forget ourselves, becoming excited when we saw bulldozers and concrete mixers, even when Nile wasn't in the car with us. Nile still likes them, but now he likes superheroes and Legos, too, and he no longer shouts *There's another one! There's another one!* at cranes and dump trucks while we're driving. It's strange for me to think of him as an adult, as someone with a bank account and a job and a relationship to manage, instead of somebody who just wants to push toy trucks around the floor. It feels like, whoever that adult is, it won't be the same person Nile is now. It'll be somebody else entirely.

"What state is Iowa in?" Nile asks from the backseat.

"Iowa is its own state," I tell him. "Some of the towns are called Waterloo, and Maxwell, and Des Moines."

"Oh," Nile says. "Is there a New York City in Iowa?"

"No," I say. "New York City is in New York City."

"Oh. What are some other towns in Iowa?"

I launch into a list that sounds like it's lifted from a Johnny Cash song. "There's Coon Rapids, Cedar Rapids, Cedar Falls, Sioux Falls, Sioux City, Iowa City, Iowa Center, State Center."

"Do they have any subway trains?"

"No. Iowa only has small cities, baby."

"Awwwwwww!" Nile roars.

I point out the cornfield on the right side of the road and the soybean field on the left, and show Nile the difference. How the soybean plants are bushy and leafy and close to the ground, how the corn is tall and stalky, with leaves that are just as green as those of the soybean plants, but dryer-looking somehow. I always wonder how farmers decide which to plant. The prices of the two crops must be constantly shifting in relation to one another; otherwise, everybody would plant one or the other.

"Can we eat that corn?" Nile asks.

"Probably not," I say. "Most of the corn out here is either feed corn or seed corn. That means it's used to grow other plants, or it's used to feed pigs and cows. Do you want to eat pig food?"

"Yuck."

"Hey, did I tell you about the job I had in high school? I detasseled corn. That means I walked all the way up and down the fields and picked the top part off of the cornstalk."

"Did you see any tractors rumbling by?" Nile asks.

"Sometimes," I say. "But mostly I just saw corn. I spent so much time walking through the corn leaves that I saw them when I closed my eyes at night."

Nile asks whether we'll be staying with both Alice and my Grandma Wilson when we get to Waterloo, and I explain that, while we'll see Grandma Wilson, we're only staying at Alice's house. We can't visit my Grandma Wilson, I tell Nile, because my father lives with her.

"Oh," Nile says. "Is your daddy nice to Grandma Wilson?"

"I honestly don't know," I say. "Maybe he is. Maybe he helps her out."

"Is he nice to Grandma Alice?"

"No. Grandma Alice doesn't like him."

"It's good that Grandma Alice doesn't like him."

"Yeah."

"Nobody likes your father," Nile says.

"Some people might," I say.

"Only you like your father."

"I don't like him."

"Because he's mean," Nile says, remembering. "Maybe if I talked to him, I would say, 'Good morning, what's your name?' But then he wouldn't answer me, right? Like, if you said hello to your father when you were a kid, he wouldn't say hello back to you?"

"If you said hello to my father," I tell Nile, "he would probably say it back."

"Oh," Nile says. "Then what did he do that was mean?"

I take a breath, trying to decide how to answer. If my father had beaten me with a whip or a hammer, or if he'd come home drunk every night and kicked the shit out of me, these would be easy things to explain to Nile. But that wasn't the problem. The problem was that he wasn't there. And when he was there, he was useless to me. The problem was that he skipped out on the hard, necessary work of raising his sons.

"You want to know one mean thing about my daddy?" I say.

Nile leans forward in his booster seat. "What?"

"You know how some people like Mommy have dark brown skin?" I say, measuring out my words. "And remember, how those people are called 'black'? My daddy doesn't like black people."

It's entirely possible that I'm taking things too far here. A week ago, Nile hadn't even heard of "black people" and "white people," and now I'm telling him that his own grandfather is a racist. I still don't know where this line is, still don't know when to be honest with Nile and when to protect him from the truth.

"Oh!" Nile exclaims. "What did your father do when black people or brown people walked by?"

I think of the things my father said to me, back when I still spoke to him. He referred to MTV as "NTV" because there were, in his opinion, too many black people on the channel. He told me that, in his experience, blacks couldn't be trusted. He told me that the "niggers" were responsible for getting him hooked on meth.

"Sometimes my daddy calls black people names," I tell Nile.

"Like what?"

"They're bad names. I don't want to say them."

"Oh," Nile says. "Well, if he saw a black or a brown woman like Mommy, would he say all the bad names to her?"

"He might call her names," I say. "Or he might just not like her, because she's black."

"And she would be like, 'Oh, please stop,'" Nile says. "Like that?"

"Probably like that."

It does not escape my attention that Nile has chosen Belzie, rather than himself, as the "black or brown" person facing discrimination in this hypothetical scenario. Although we've discussed racism several times now, I still don't think it's occurred to Nile that someone might discriminate one day against *him*. I'm glad for that.

"So," I say. "I don't think my father is very nice. What do you think?"

"I don't think he's very nice."

"So we don't want to see him. And so we won't go to Grandma Wilson's house. Okay?"

After my conversation with Belzie, I wonder if I'm trying to convince Nile here, or if I'm really trying to convince myself. I allow myself to imagine, just for a moment, walking through the door of that old house. I imagine seeing my father in the flesh for the first time in forever. As soon as I see his face in my mind's eye, the tape cuts out. I literally cannot imagine what we might have to say to one another.

"Okay," Nile says. He sits silent for a minute, and then he asks, "Daddy? Are there any bullet trains in Iowa?"

"No, baby," I tell him. "There aren't any bullet trains in Iowa."

. . .

The lazy, muddy Mississippi River half-heartedly reflects a blue sky and fluffy white clouds as we cross the bridge into Iowa. A sign says, "The People of Iowa Welcome You," but then, as though it can't make up its mind about what it wants to say, it adds, "Iowa: Fields of Opportunities." This is Nile's first time in my home state, but I come back around once a year, for friends' weddings or college football games. I lived in Iowa until I was twenty-two, but subtracting the two years when I lived in Massachusetts with my mom and brothers as a kid, I spent an even two decades here. Now, I've been gone long enough that the Hawkeye State has become shrouded for me in myth, built up as a sort of paradise where everybody is always nice to each other and there's never any traffic. Those two things are, in fact, largely true, but I have to remind myself that the wind chill in the winter routinely reaches into the negative double digits, and that there's a total of something like seventeen black people in the entire state.

I tell Nile to start looking out the window for his first Iowa barn.

"There's one!" he says immediately.

I squint out at the horizon. "I don't see it."

"There!" Nile says. "There! There!"

"That's two grain silos," I tell him.

"Oh."

We begin seeing signs for Herbert Hoover's presidential

library in West Branch. I've never been, and we don't have time to stop, but I tell Nile the little bit I know about Hoover, which pretty much boils down to the fact that most people think he was a lousy president on account of his response to the Great Depression, but that he was a decent man who'd done a lot of work feeding the world's poor before entering the White House. This leads to a discussion about the current presidential election, which leads to a discussion about how there's never been a female president. And *that* leads to a discussion about all the different things women weren't allowed to do throughout history, which leads to a barrage of questions from Nile about whether women were allowed to drive a number of very specific different types of trucks. When I tell him that, no, women weren't allowed to drive city buses or fire engines or tow trucks, he shouts, "WHAT?!?!" in comical, exaggerated tones.

I spot some exit signs for tiny towns whose names I vaguely recognize from high-school sports. Whenever I tell anyone where I'm from, I spit out the population as part of the town's name – *Maxwell, Iowa, population 800* – so that people don't apologize for not having heard of it. Physically, the area that's considered "in town" has a circumference of almost exactly two miles, making Maxwell only slightly larger than the Jackie O Reservoir in Central Park. It must be terribly inefficient, building out water lines and sewers and roads and classrooms for such a little pocket of people tucked away from the rest of the world, but the entire state is dotted with these little hamlets. When I moved to Massachusetts as a kid, I was amazed at the way one town led directly into the other, without miles of cornfields to separate them.

For school and sports, Maxwell combined efforts with other nearby towns. The schools were consolidated with Collins, a town of around 500, which sat five miles from

Maxwell, and still, my graduating class had only forty-two kids, and two of those were foreign exchange students. (We always seemed to have more than our fair share of kids from Germany and Australia and Peru, since a handful of local families volunteered to host over and over again, relying on the modest stipends that accompanied the students.) For sports, we joined with Baxter, which was eighteen miles from Maxwell, and together the three towns were able to supply enough wiry teenage bodies to fill out the football and track teams. For niche sports like wrestling, though, we had to rope in yet another school, Colo-NESCO, itself an unholy amalgamation of towns so small and remote that anthropologists might consider them "uncontacted." (The reason "NESCO" is in all-caps is because it's short for "Northeast Story County," and includes towns like Zearing, pop. 550, and McCallsburg, pop. 330.) Some of these little communities sit farther from each other than the distance between Baltimore and Washington, D.C., and yet the wrestlers boarded buses after school each day and traveled from site to site for the chance to contract ringworm.

When I was in high school, I hated where I was from, and couldn't wait to leave. But now that I'm not trapped there, I find the existence of such a small, weird community more entertaining than depressing. Maxwell is a place where Stan the Junk Man, a borderline legendary character who lived across from the town park, was rumored to bathe once a year during Old Settlers, bringing a bar of soap with him into the Indian Creek and washing himself in the light of the moon. Maxwell is a place where the high school offered classes with titles like Farm Accounting, and where there was an annual Drive Your Tractor to School Day. Maxwell is a place where, after an afternoon of bailing hay for a classmate's father, I witnessed a male dog raping a tomcat while two farmhands cheered the dog on, hollering, "Get him, Tippie!"

Up ahead, just off the highway, the Iowa 80 truck stop outside of Walcott comes into view, its massive parking lot full of 18-wheelers. A gigantic digital sign advertises "Sparkling Clean Showers" one second and "Quick Haircuts" the next.

"Nile," I say. "Do you want to see the world's largest truck stop?"

"Yeah!" Nile says, pointing out the window. "Look at all those trucks! Can I look at all of them?"

"Some of them." I click on my turn signal and slow for the exit. "We can only spend a few minutes inside, okay? We have to get back on the road to see Grandma Alice."

"Well, can I sit inside them?"

"I don't think they let you sit inside the trucks."

We park and get out of the Black Racer, and instantly I'm slapped by the heat. The temperature is only in the mid-80s, but it's that particular Iowa heat, where the sun instantly roasts your neck, and the air is so thick and humid you could plant corn in it. We step into the air conditioning of the truck stop, which is equal parts auto parts store, hospital gift shop, and church bazaar. Here are some things you can buy at the world's largest truck stop, if you are so inclined: Iowa Hawkeyes apparel, Precious Moments figurines, Christian-themed belt buckles, sheepskin carseat covers, a toy big rig that says "I Love Jesus," a 24-inch television, aftermarket headlights, military patches, dream catchers, decorative fire hydrants, Star Wars toys, footwear from a surprisingly large shoe selection, an acoustic guitar, or any one of many thousands of pre-owned DVDs.

Nile makes a beeline for the truck-parts section, mesmerized by the disembodied steering wheels and chrome stacks available for purchase. The cab of a yellow big rig slowly spins on a rotating section of the floor, and it turns out that

Nile is allowed to sit in this truck after all. He clambers up the steps and grips the wheel, his feet nowhere near touching the pedals, then gets out again and wanders the aisles, gaping up at taillights and fenders. He calls this section of the store the "truck museum," and although there is an *actual* truck museum onsite, I don't tell Nile about it, because we need to get going. I give him a two-minute warning, then coax him back outside with a promise to walk over to the truck lot.

Outside, we look out together at the ocean of big rigs, and I imagine the hundreds of truckers who must be napping in their cabs. Then I imagine the trucks without their drivers, replaced by automation. There are many reasons I wanted to take this trip with Nile now, but one of them is the rise of self-driving cars, which I imagine will be everywhere by the time he grows up. I tend to think that automation is a good thing (the napping truckers may disagree with me), but it means that, by the time Nile is my age, these sorts of wandering road trips may be a relic of the past. Already, smartphone apps and GPS have changed the way people travel, to the point where I felt almost precious buying the hard copy of the road atlas before the trip.

After barely a minute in the parking lot, I'm working up a sweat, and I guide Nile back to the Black Racer.

"Daddy?" Nile says as I buckle him into his booster seat. "I'm going to ask you something else about women in the olden times. Could any women be truck drivers?"

"I don't think so, baby," I tell him. "All the truck drivers were men."

"What?!" Nile protests. "Come on! Women couldn't drive military trucks? Or they couldn't drive campers? Or they couldn't drive even a single 18-wheeler that could go fast, fast, fast down the highway?"

"Nope," I tell him. "Women weren't allowed in the

military. In fact, a long time ago, women couldn't even have jobs. They just had to do whatever their husbands told them to do."

"WHAT???!"

. . .

I'd planned to skip Iowa City and head straight to Waterloo, but our progress is slower than I expected, and we hit my old college town right at lunchtime. I pull off the interstate and drive toward campus. "You know something special about Iowa City?" I say. "I lived here for four years and went to college."

"Boston College?" Nile asks, naming Belzie's alma mater.

"No," I say. "It's called the University of Iowa."

"You mean Iowa College," Nile says.

"That's not its name."

"That's just what I call it."

At the edge of town, we pass Parkview Church, an evangelical congregation where, during my freshman year, I attended a Thursday night program for students called 24:7, named after some obscure Bible verse. I traveled with the group to Denver during spring break for a service trip, sorting through clothing donations and working in a soup kitchen, but over time my faith slipped away, and I quit going to church. There wasn't any one event that made me stop believing. I just found that the things I'd believed my entire life didn't hold up once I finally allowed myself to test them against critical thought. People in Maxwell warned me that this would happen if I went to school in Iowa City, and they were right. I became a godless liberal.

We drive by the edge of campus, passing a couple of dorms where I lived for a year apiece, and then we park at the Old Capitol Mall downtown. The mall was nearing death when I was in school, but has been given a second life by the university, which appears to be renting out around two-thirds of the available space. Nile and I step out into the heat (according to a bank sign, the temperature has crept up to 87 degrees) and make our way through the brick pedestrian mall, passing through a gauntlet of undergrad bars. I actually had my first drink not in Iowa City, but in my friend Brice's dorm room at his community college in Ottumwa, where we poured Smirnoff Ice into empty bottles of Gatorade Frost to fool his RA, and I let the fuzzy warmth of the alcohol numb my brain and help me forget about the girl who'd dumped me. But the University of Iowa always ranks near the top of the national "party school" lists, and the downtown bars had absurd drink specials, like $1 domestic pitchers and 25-cent Captain-and-Cokes, making it easy to get drunk for next to nothing. At the end of one semester, the campus newspaper where I worked ran an ad with a coupon for a free pint of Leinenkugel's Honey Weiss. There was a limit of one free drink per customer, but the coupon was redeemable at a dozen different bars within walking distance of each other, and I cut out 200 of the coupons and organized an informal bar crawl where twenty of us all got wasted for free.

Everybody drank. But not everybody drank hard liquor alone while watching cable news on school nights. Not everybody went out to the bars all seven nights during finals week. Not everybody was already a regular at a townie tavern, drinking with men who'd been sitting on the same stools for decades. I kept drinking even after it stopped feeling good. I wanted to obliterate my consciousness, to get the part of my brain that constantly reminds me of all of my shortcomings to just *shut the fuck up* for a minute. At one point, I forgot what it felt like to wake up without a hangover.

Nile and I eat at India Cafe, where I first tasted Indian food during my first week of college. The food is half the price of the meal we had on the first night of our trip, in Massachusetts, but twice as good, and Nile and I fill up on tandoori chicken, chicken tikka masala, and pakoras, too tired and hungry to say much as we eat.

"Did you know that Daddy was born in Iowa City?" I ask Nile after I've finished my meal.

"Nuh," Nile grunts.

"Right over that way." I gesture to the west. "Over in the university hospital."

Nile just stares at me, his eyes drooping.

My parents lived in Waterloo when my mom was pregnant with me, but they didn't have health insurance, and so when it was time for me to be born, my father drove my mother eighty miles southeast to the teaching hospital here, and then turned around and drove straight back to Waterloo because he had to be at work. According to my mom's telling, she was staying at a "home for unwed mothers" in Iowa City when her water broke, and then she wandered around the hospital campus with her jacket tied around her waist, asking for directions to the maternity ward. None of this fully makes sense to me. Why was she already at the "home for unwed mothers" when she went into labor? Why was she allowed to stay there at all, given that she wasn't "unwed" (or even yet, for that matter, a mother)? Why didn't the home have a shuttle to drive the unwed mothers to the hospital, rather than forcing the poor women to seek out the labor rooms on their own, in the cold, wearing wet pants? But that's the story my mom tells.

I had to stay in the hospital for observation. According to my mother, I was a "blue baby," but when I ask her what this means, she just repeats it at me, louder, like I'm stupid.

"You were a BLUE baby!!" My mom couldn't afford a hotel, and so my father came and picked her up, and they left me there in the hospital by myself for nine days. I was the second grandchild on my father's side of the family, but no one came to see me until Papa, my dad's dad, finally drove my mom back down to Iowa City on that ninth day to bring me home. "Well," my mother says now, when I press her about this. "That's just how things were back then, I guess."

My mom, originally from Massachusetts, moved out to Iowa to be with my dad after she learned that she was pregnant with me. They'd met a year earlier, when they were both shiftless young drifters hanging out in Florida. My mom saw my father carrying drums off the back of a truck into a bar, and she was attracted to him because she thought he was in a rock band. But it turned out that he was just helping some dudes unload some drums from a truck, and this – this! – is why I even exist.

After she learned that my dad wasn't a drummer, and after the haze of the drugs they were both doing in Florida wore off, the thing that drew my mother to him was his family. His mom and dad were divorced, the same as her parents, and they didn't have a lot of money or particularly impressive jobs, but my mom liked the way they treated her. Her own father was stern and unapproachable, and her mother was aloof, but she found that she could sit at the kitchen table with my dad's mom or dad and just casually chat about her day over a cup of coffee. That's all it took to win her over. Some coffee and light conversation.

This amazes me to think about. Thirty-four years ago, my mom was lost in the world, and to find her way, she ran toward the same thing I've spent my life running away from. She ran toward my family.

...

Nile gets a second wind when we get back in the car, but eating has only made me more tired, and I have to hunch over my steering wheel and periodically shake my head back and forth to stay awake on Interstate 380, which is possibly the most hypnotic stretch of asphalt in the entire country. We're nearing the city limits of Cedar Rapids, home to a huge Quaker Oats factory, and the car fills with the faint scent of burning oatmeal.

"What should we use to make a tower?" Nile asks from the back seat, his voice energetic and chipper. "A crane, a wrecking ball, or a bulldozer?"

He's invented a game where he asks me multiple-choice questions about hypothetical construction scenarios, but I keep losing focus. "The crane?" I say, stifling a yawn.

Nile makes little presto-change-o sounds with his mouth, and in the rearview I can see him waving his hands in front of his face. "The tower is all built!" he announces. "Now a man is stuck on a wire. Which emergency equipment should we use? The bucket truck, the ladder truck, or the bouncy emergency net?"

"What do we need it for again?" I blink my eyes a few times, trying to keep them from shutting all the way. "I'm sorry, I need to focus on the road. Why don't you tell me a story?"

"Once upon a time," Nile begins, and then immediately starts over. "This is going to be about a big, big city. Once upon a time, there was a big, big city, and it had big towers, and some zoos, and merry-go-rounds, and taxis, and um, um, Uber rides. But the thing that a boy mostly wanted in the city was ..."

Already I'm tuning him out, trying to keep my attention

on the road. Belzie and I have read thousands of books to Nile, and he's internalized the conventions of narrative – the dramatic pauses, the stresses, the elongation and clipping meant to imbue otherwise pedestrian vocabulary with a sense of excitement. If I don't listen to his stories too closely, it's easy to be impressed, to think that he possesses the cadences of a natural-born storyteller. But then I tune back in, and it's all nonsense.

"There was a baby in the pool that started crying," Nile says. "It cried louder and louder! The mom and the boy DASHED out of the elevator and RACED out of the hotel!"

Just as I'm wondering how an infant made its way into this narrative, the baby is gone. "The mom and the boy waited at the bus stop, but the bus would not come," Nile continues. "The bus just didn't. And then a strange thing happened. The bus did come!"

His stories are full of this sort of thing: a minor problem that presents itself out of nowhere, followed by an immediate resolution. He understands that stories should be centered around conflict, I think, but instead of giving the listener a steady drumbeat of complication and development leading up to a climax, he just offers up one miniature crisis after another.

Nile goes on like this for a solid hour (at one point going into great detail about an argument this fictional boy has with his mother about whether she should put jelly on his peanut butter sandwich), until we at last reach the outskirts of Waterloo.

"We're almost at Grandma Alice's house," I tell him. I point out minor landmarks – a stone quarry, a shopping mall. "There's a Panera," I say. "There's Subway."

"Oh!" Nile says. "They have a subway here!"

"Subway the restaurant," I clarify. "Not a subway train."

Alice has lived with her brother Harry since I graduated from high school, and although I lived in Waterloo until I was five and have had family here all my life, I still can't really get a read on the town. It seems both quaint and gritty, somehow, one foot planted in the bland, strip-mall sprawl of suburbia, and the other in the grimy desperation of the forgotten industrial Midwest. Fifteen percent of the population is African-American, making the city one of the most diverse in all of Iowa, but I've never seen a black person in Alice's or Grandma Wilson's neighborhoods. I know that Waterloo has a sizable Bosnian population, but I have no idea how this came to be, or how it's working out. I've heard Alice claim that the teenagers here are constantly killing each other, but I've glanced at the city's crime statistics, and they show that Waterloo's murder rate has hovered between "one per year" and "slightly more than one per year" for more than a decade. Once, my father, who's lived in Waterloo nearly all his life, referred to Cedar Rapids as the "Emerald City" for its supposed opulence, and it probably tells you something about Waterloo that the people here are jealous of a place that smells like burning oatmeal.

Harry's house is nestled among dozens of nondescript 1970s ranches with lawns the color of green Crayola crayons, just a couple of blocks from one of Waterloo's two public high schools. I pull the Black Racer into the doublewide concrete driveway of the tiny beige house, and Nile and I get out and enter through the garage, which reeks of stale cigarette smoke. The door is never locked, but I give it a perfunctory knock and then let myself into the kitchen.

The counters are a mess. Years ago, Alice used to clean people's houses for money, and she earned a reputation as a neat freak for harassing near strangers about the dust collecting on the picture frames in their own homes. But the kitchen is littered with junk mail and bills and forgotten to-do lists.

Batteries and binder clips lie scattered next to unsent greeting cards. A yellow highlighter stands on its end beside the sink, next to bottles of Goof Off and Windex.

The faint sound of the television wafts in from the living room, but Alice is sitting on a lawn chair outside on the back deck, visible through the sliding glass doors. She's smoking and looking off into the distance, wearing nothing but a long, tattered white V-neck tee shirt and a pair of brown slippers, holding her cigarette in one hand and a dog's leash in the other. The dog is a brown-and-white spaniel of some sort. I don't recognize it.

I stand for a moment watching Alice. Her skin used to be the color of brown leather from the hours she spent lying in tanning beds and baking in the sun, but it's faded over the years to the lifeless color of Silly Putty, sallow somehow without quite being pale. Deep lines crease her face and neck, and veins bulge in her hands and ankles. On her stick-skinny arms and legs, the skin looks like it's melting away.

After I graduated from high school, I thought I'd never want to see Alice again. I thought I could never forgive her for the way she made me feel when I lived with her. But after I went to college, our entire relationship changed. Just as suddenly as she had started hating me, she seemed to stop. I don't know if she sensed that she wouldn't be able to control me now that I was an adult, or if it was as simple as the fact that she could only stand me when she didn't have to see my face every day, but it was as though she turned off a faucet that she'd left running for seven years. She started bragging about me to anyone who would listen. She started to love me again.

After I moved to New York, when I told Alice I was dating a black girl, the first thing she said was, "You're not going to marry her, are you?" I told Alice that I didn't know, that Belzie and I had only been dating a couple of months. "Well,"

Alice guffawed into the phone. "I don't want any gray-striped grandchildren."

Alice is a lifelong Democrat, and has always claimed that she can't be racist because she adored the "colored" maid who worked for her father when she was a child. When I lived with her, she called Asian people UFOs (short for "Ugly Fucking Orientals"), and if we passed a Korean family in the supermarket, she would wait until they were out of earshot and then squint her eyes and curl her lips to create mock buckteeth and let loose a torrent of ching-chong-ding-dong gibberish. She used the N-word liberally, and told jokes about Buckwheat from the Little Rascals getting his dick sucked. But as soon as it became clear that I was serious about Belzie, Alice forgot her objections. She flew to Boston for our wedding and bawled during the ceremony. On the phone, she pestered me to "hurry up and make some little Tiger Woodses." When Nile was born, she fell in love, first with the idea of him, and then, after she'd met him, with the boy himself. When he was two years old, I received a package from Alice in the mail. I opened it and unfolded its contents, slightly bewildered. It was a blanket she'd had made, with a huge, blown-up picture of Nile's smiling, pillowy-cheeked face on it.

I take a breath and slide open the door to the deck. "Hi, Alice."

It takes her a moment to register our presence, and then Alice blinks up at me in surprise, as though she hasn't been expecting us. "Oh!" she says. "Oh my God. Hi, Nile!"

Nile hides behind my legs from the spaniel, which has come over to sniff at his feet. "Grandma Alice," he says, squirming. "I didn't know you had a dog."

"He's scared," I explain.

"Oh, he won't hurt you, honey," Alice says.

I scratch the dog behind the ear and then lean over so that

I can give Alice a hug without her having to stand up. "How are you doing?"

"Well," Alice says. "I just crawled out of bed. Hey, shut that door."

The spaniel is tugging at its leash, trying to get back inside. "I will," I say. "If the dog will let me."

"Peanut!" Alice says. "Come here, Peanut."

The dog moves out of the way, and I slide the door shut. "The dog's name is Peanut?"

"Grandma Alice?" Nile says. He sits on the chair across from her, and I drop my weight onto the lawn chair beside her, grateful for the opportunity to close my eyes without risking a car accident. "Can I show you the sticker book thing that I made?"

"Yes, you can," Alice says, suddenly energetic. She points to his electric blue sneakers. "Oh, I love your shoes!"

Nile leafs through the oversized book of cling stickers that Belzie bought for him before the trip. "This one, it's got lots of cars and trucks. And this one, there's a train going by."

"Whose dog?" I ask Alice.

"My niece's. He's only here for a few days." Alice stubs out her cigarette and lights a new one. "Do you have laundry?"

"Some. I'll do it tomorrow." I nod to the cigarette. "Smoking again?"

"It's the only vice I have," Alice says. "I'm going to keep it. Ha ha!"

"Okay." I laugh along with her and stand up. If I sit here for too long, I'll never want to get up, and so I force myself to go unload the car, stopping by the living room first to say hello to Harry, who's watching a women's soccer game in the living room. He's a retired cop, in his early seventies – a couple of years younger than Alice – and although he's never been unkind to me, we never have much to say to one another. He tells me that his eldest son recently visited from Colorado, and asks me how long we've been on the road, and then I go outside to get the bags.

I make two trips, and when I come back inside, Nile is walking around the dining room, chatting away on a cordless phone. "And then we saw two big waterfalls," he tells the person on the other line. "And we didn't go on the go-karts, because they were too loud, but we went on the Ferris wheel instead, and then we went to Chicago and saw Mommy and Peanut and ate unusual pizza."

I set the suitcases next to the door to the basement. "Who's he talking to?"

"Willy," Alice says, giving her private nickname for my Grandma Wilson.

"But I'm not going to stay at your house," Nile says, "because Daddy's father lives with you."

"Nile!" I say, unable to stifle a laugh. "Don't talk to her about that right now, okay?"

"Okay, Daddy."

"Oh, she knows," Alice says. "She knows why you won't go over there."

"Still," I say.

In fact, my Grandma Wilson may not know why we're not coming to her house. As she's gotten older, she sometimes seems to forget that my father and I don't speak to one another. And even since long before that, our relationship has been based on the fact that we don't talk about my father. Grandma Wilson never pressured me to see him or speak to him when I didn't want to, and I never asked her how she could provide food and shelter to a grown man who wouldn't even provide for his own children. I love my Grandma Wilson, but as I suspect is the case in many families, our relationship

depends on a certain amount of pretending that things aren't
the way they are.

Alice hands me a small package. "These are the scan cards
I was telling you about. Let me show you how they work."

She's been talking about these for weeks. They're RFID-
blocking cards that you stick in your wallet to prevent thieves
from remotely stealing your credit card credentials. I don't
know if this sort of digital pickpocketing is actually a thing,
but I do know that none of my credit cards have RFID chips.
But it's easier to go along than to try to explain this to Alice.
She bought them, I suspect, from the home shopping channel.
Shortly after Belzie and I moved into our house, an $800 La-
Z-Boy recliner that Alice ordered from the television arrived
on our porch. After we returned it, a $150 set of tacky flat-
ware showed up. There's no stopping her.

"Grandma Wilson," Nile says into the phone. "I heard
that I was going to a restaurant with you tomorrow."

"You know where we should go?" Alice says to me.
"Pizza Ranch. My God, is that goooood!"

"I've already got it planned out with Aunt Jane," I say.
"We're meeting at Chuck E. Cheese, so that Nile has something to do besides listen to us talk."

Nile finishes up on the phone, and Alice takes it from him.
"Calvin says we're supposed to go to Chuck E. Cheese," she
says into the receiver. "Now, would you rather get together
for lunch or for dinner?"

"It's already planned," I tell her. "Five o'clock at Chuck
E. Cheese. Jane has it down."

"Oh!" Alice says into the phone. "Jane already has it
written down, that we're going out for Chinese – "

"Chuck E. Cheese!" I say.

"Chuck E. Cheese," Alice says, nodding. "Chuck E.
Cheese, Chuck E. Cheese."

. . .

Alice has only been out of bed for around an hour, but she and Nile both want to lie down, and so I set him up with the TV in her bedroom. He isn't interested in any of the shows playing on the kids' channels, but Alice's ancient television has a built-in VCR, and I go down to the basement to find a movie that Nile might like. There's a cabinet full of all our old VHS tapes from the nineties – "Only the Lonely," "King Ralph," "The Firm," "My Best Friend's Wedding" – and among them I find the animated 1970s adaptation of E.B. White's "Charlotte's Web."

I bring the tape upstairs and pop it into the television, and Nile props himself up on his elbows at the foot of the bed and stares wide-eyed up at the screen. Alice hasn't yet put her laundered sheets back on her bed, and so she lies on the bare mattress and pillow with a blanket pulled up to her chest, petting the dog with her curled, arthritic fingers. She isn't in the same form as when I used to lie in bed and watch TV with her, but still, seeing her with Nile like this brings me back to when I was a little boy. For the first time on the trip, I have the feeling of watching a scene from my childhood played out in front of me.

I leave them to their movie and go down to the basement, which is the same size as the entire rest of the house. One half is finished, with carpeting and a king sized bed. The unfinished side has a spartan shower stall, a washer and drier, a deep freezer, and a spare refrigerator that's stocked full of Dr. Pepper. Magneted to the refrigerator are two laminated clippings of my college graduation picture, which Alice submitted to the weekly newspaper that covers Maxwell and a few other small towns, printing stories on such riveting topics as who had whom over to dinner. The freezer is filled with many of multiples of the things that Alice buys on sale at Fareway: eight-slice boxes of cheesy toast, containers of Cool Whip, pounds and pounds of salted butter.

Toward the back of the basement sit several racks of Alice's clothes, which have spilled over into the finished side, as well. Most of the items still have the tags on them, and on the finished side of the basement alone, the untouched blouses and blazers and pants take up four big racks, crowding up the room. Alice isn't a hoarder, but rather, a compulsive shopper. She's been sober from alcohol for around forty years, but she's still addicted to spending money. When I was in high school, she would raid my bank account, taking out hundreds of dollars to pay off her credit cards, making empty promises to pay me back. Once, I opened a separate account that only I had access to, but Alice found out (Maxwell is a small, small town) and made me shut it down. Now, she lives off her Social Security check, and although the money isn't much, her expenses are even less. She sends me a few hundred dollars at Christmas, and during other parts of the year to help us fund a big purchase like a new bed or a snow blower. I feel bad about taking her money, but I know that if she didn't give it to me, she'd just buy more garbage from the television, and a part of me sees it as payback for all the money she took from me when I was a teenager.

The rest of the furnished side of the basement is like a museum of our house in Maxwell, filled with all our old knick-knacks and photographs. I instantly recognize the stacked, mirrored cubes that used to sit in our living room, topped now with false flowers and a golden-framed photograph of my brothers and me, all sporting bowl cuts and wearing the colorful silk shirts that Alice insisted were the height of fashion in 1994. There are some photos of Harry's sons and Alice's other nieces and nephews scattered around the basement, but most are of my brothers and me: our school pictures, snap-shots from a trip we all took to Las Vegas, posed studio por-traits taken at Sears and Walmart.

At the far end of the basement, against the painted white cinder block wall, sits what I call "The Shrine." It's a blue trunk, draped with a floral scarf and topped with memen-tos of Alice's marriage to Papa. There's a white candle, next to a framed invitation to their wedding, which begins with the words, "This day I will marry my best friend, the one I laugh with, live for, love." There's a photograph of Papa and Alice with me when I was thirteen or fourteen years old. In it, Alice wears enormous eyeglasses and holds our pet Shih Tzu Bridgett, now long dead. She already has the teased, graying curls of an old lady, but her smiling face is plump and unwrin-kled. Papa has Coke-bottle lenses and a full head of hair that has only just begun to gray. He's smiling, but there appears to be a look – and perhaps this is just me projecting, drawing on my own knowledge of what's to come – of uncertainty on his face. They're both seated, and I'm standing behind them, smiling a dopey smile, still several years away from growing into my front teeth. On the wall, above all this, hangs a small framed embroidering of a heart with these words inside:

The Hennicks
George + Alice
September 27
1980

But the centerpiece of The Shrine is a poster-sized wed-ding portrait, taken at the Elks Lodge where Papa and Alice were married. They're both wearing white, standing at the center of a candlelit altar, gazing into each other's eyes. Papa isn't yet fifty in this photo, Alice not yet forty. It's strange to see them frozen in the happiness of this moment, totally ignorant of all the joy and the pain ahead of them. Behind them, these words are inscribed on a stone wall: "The faults of our brothers we write upon the sand, their virtues upon the tablets of love and memory."

The Shrine has been here as long as Alice has, I think. Back when we still lived in Maxwell, she kept Papa's voice on the answering machine, and when she felt lonely, she would drive to a payphone and call the house and listen to his voice. He's been gone for twenty years, and dead for three, but she's never really gotten over him.

• • •

When I was fifteen years old, after I'd been living with them for four years, Papa and Alice decided to legally adopt me. I'm still not sure why. At the time, I think they said something about "tax reasons," but I'm certain they could have claimed me as a dependent even if I wasn't legally their child. In any case, the adoption would have been merely a matter of paperwork, except that my father, who I hadn't seen in several years, contested it. This forced Papa and Alice to get a family lawyer, which must have erased any potential tax savings, but at that point, I suspect that Alice was motivated to push the issue out of pure spite.

The lawyer was a bald man with a mustache and an ill-fitting brown suit, and I had to go to his office with Papa and Alice in preparation for the adoption hearing. He told me that, when we got to court, he would ask me some basic factual questions. How long had I lived with Papa and Alice? Where did I go to school? Did I get fed every day? Then he ran through some practice questions. "Do you love your grandfather?" he said, starting off with a softball.

"Yes," I said.

"And do you love your grandmother?"

The question was meant to be a formality, but I froze. This was when Alice was telling me every day that I was a "faggot," that I was "worthless," that she wasn't my "nigger slave." I looked at Papa, who didn't meet my eyes. I looked at Alice, who laughed nervously, pretending that my pause was a joke. I looked at the lawyer, who looked back at me stone-faced.

"If I ask that question in court," he said, "the answer has to be yes."

"Then yes," I said. "The answer is yes."

On the day of the hearing, there were just six of us in the courtroom: me, Papa, Alice, the judge, the lawyer, and my father, who was representing himself. My father told the judge that he was hard of hearing in one ear, which was news to me, but the judge promised to speak up, and told my father to ask for clarification if he missed anything. The judge asked my father why he was contesting the adoption, and my father said that Alice was the problem. "I don't want my son to be raised by a woman of such low character," he said.

It doesn't seem like this can be how things actually happened, but in my memory, I'm the only one to take the stand, the only one to sit in the witness chair and get peppered with questions. I don't remember my grandparents having to explain why they wanted to adopt me, and I don't remember my father detailing his issues with Alice's character. In my memory, I'm the only one sitting in front of everybody, forced to explain myself.

The judge didn't ask me to place my hand on the Bible and swear to tell the truth, which made me feel better about the lie I was about to tell about loving Alice. But it turned out not to matter. The lawyer, probably thinking it was implicit anyway, and not wanting the judge to see me hesitate, never asked whether I loved my grandparents. Instead, he asked me the same basic questions he'd asked in his office: how long I'd lived with Papa and Alice, how old I was. His final question was about the sorts of things I was involved with at school, and I listed everything I could think of, even the stuff I'd done just to get my picture in the yearbook: track, cross country, chorus, the school play, the school musical, a group called Students Opposed to Drugs and Alcohol, another group called the Miles Per Gallon Club. I kept rattling them off, trying unconsciously, I suppose, to impress my father, who after years with zero contact was suddenly sitting right in front of me, dressed in a too-big button-down shirt tucked into faded blue jeans, staring up at me with his beady eyes.

The lawyer had only spent five or six minutes questioning me when he sat back down. The case was open-and-shut. I had no relationship with my father and didn't want one. Nothing my father said was going to convince the judge to block the adoption.

My father stood up to question me. He's a nervous little man with a wiry frame and gaunt cheeks, always clearing his throat and darting his eyes from one thing to another. I don't know how many questions he asked me. I only remember the last one. "Did you ever think," he said, "that maybe, growing up, you only got one side of the story?"

I looked at him. It was odd, almost surreal, to see him standing there in person, this man who I'd built up in my mind as a villain. What did I really know about him? That he'd broken into our house and burned holes in my mother's underwear. That he'd woken her in the middle of the night countless times with phone calls from pay phones where he just breathed heavily into the receiver. That he'd quit every job he'd ever had so he could get out of paying child support. But I'd heard all of that from my mom and from Alice. I'd never really gotten to know him.

I swallowed a lump in my throat. "Maybe."

• • •

After Nile and Alice finish their movie, we head out to get some things from the grocery store and to pick up Chinese takeout for dinner. At Fareway, I buy some KIND bars, seltzer water, and Diet Pepsi, and Alice loads up our cart with sugar: handfuls of Snickers, a two-pound bag of Twizzler Pull-N-Peels, a package of something called Chocolate Kreme Kurls. "I went to a fiftieth wedding anniversary this summer," she tells me. "You know how there's always a big string of frosting left over on the sheet after the cake is all gone? Well, I kept cating that frosting, and then one of the waitresses took an entire cake and put it on another plate and gave me the sheet, and I ate all that frosting, too. Ha ha!"

Back at the house, we eat the Chinese food in a zombified stupor. My General Tso's is the same bland, mushy stuff that I had in Michigan, and I feel stupid for making the same mistake twice in four days. Harry takes his dinner in the living room in front of the TV, Nile and I sit at the dining room table, and Alice eats standing over the kitchen sink, feeding more of her sweet and sour chicken to the yippy, jumping spaniel than she puts in her own mouth. Nile's eyes are so tired they look practically inhuman, and he occasionally shouts out nonsense phrases. "Hey, chicken dog man!" he yells to no one. "You're a two-chicken squeezey dog!" By seven o'clock, he's begging me to put him to bed.

It's still light outside, but the basement is dark, and I lie down with Nile in the king bed and try to read him a chapter from "The Boxcar Children." The four siblings spend several pages gathering clams and seaweed, and I find myself wondering why I ever thought these books were interesting. Nile, thrashing about in the sheets, only barely listens.

"Stop, stop, stop," I say. "Put your head on the pillow."

Nile spins under the sheets, wrapping them around his body like a mummy. "Hey, pillow dog man! Your pillow makes too many dogs!"

I close the book. "If you keep acting up, I'm going to make you sleep on the floor."

"I don't want to sleep on the floor," Nile says, his voice suddenly serious. "The floor is too hard."

I rush through the rest of his bedtime, doing the singing and the counting and asking him about the best part of his day and what he's going to dream about. The entire time, he's rolling around in the blankets and slapping at his pillow.

"Stop." I let out a frustrated sigh. "Stop, stop!"

"What's the matter, Daddy?" Nile says.

I put my arm around him and guide his head onto my shoulder. "Nothing's the matter. We're both just tired."

"Daddy," Nile says. "You wouldn't really make me sleep on the floor, right? That was just for pretend?"

"Yeah, baby." I yawn, then put my hand on his head and run my fingers through his curls. "That was just pretend. Daddy wouldn't really do anything mean to you, would I?"

"No." Nile says the word with total conviction, and then he's quiet for a moment. I think he's drifting off to sleep, but then he says, "Daddy, did you know that we saw lots of big rigs on the highway?"

"Mmm," I say.

"And Daddy?" Nile says. "The world's biggest truck stop isn't only a truck stop. It's also a truck museum, with a yellow truck that you can sit inside. Right?"

"Right," I say. "You can say one more thing, and then no more talking."

"Okay." Nile thinks for a moment, trying to choose the best option among all the truck-related thoughts bouncing around inside his head. "If you had sat inside that yellow truck, you would have had so much fun. How come you didn't sit in it?"

"I wanted you to have all the fun," I say.

"Oh," Nile replies. "But everybody can have fun."

"We'll all have fun tomorrow," I say. "No more talking."

"Okay. Goodnight, Daddy."

"Goodnight, baby. I love you."

I kiss the top of Nile's head, and he falls asleep in an instant. I sit up in bed for a bit with my laptop, looking online to see if there's anything fun to do with him tomorrow. There's a water park in town, but I don't want to waste the money on tickets if Nile won't go on any of the slides. I remember a playground that I loved as a boy, set up to look like an Old West ghost town, but when I try to find it, I discover that it was torn down years ago. It might be better to have a lazy day anyway, to let Nile rest up before the last leg of our trip.

Looking at the city on Google Maps, I see my Grandma Wilson's neighborhood a couple of miles from where Alice lives, and I drag the little icon down and look at her house with Street View. The house is a ranch not unlike Harry's, complete with the garage entrance leading into the kitchen, three small bedrooms on the ground level, and a mostly finished basement. According to Street View, there's still a basketball hoop in the driveway. The tree in the front yard has more than doubled in size since I last saw it, and now it towers over the roof of the house. The garage door is open, with a boxy gray car parked inside, but I don't see any people. The curtains in the windows are all drawn shut.

Then I realize what I'm doing, and I get a little embarrassed, even though I'm here by myself. What I'm doing is trying to catch a glimpse of my father.

I haven't thought about him all day, other than when I

talked about him with Nile, and it's only just now occurred to me how physically close we are to him. At this very moment, he's probably sitting in my Grandma Wilson's basement across town, staring at a computer screen, just like I am. I open up a web browser and type his name into the search bar, something I do a few times a year, usually on nights like this, when I'm sitting up awake while everyone else sleeps.

I never know what I'm hoping to find.

There are several Rick Hennicks on Facebook and LinkedIn and Twitter, but none of them are my father. I can't find any record of the time when two men held him in a house overnight, occasionally beating him with a hammer (the details are fuzzy, but I've always assumed a drug debt was involved). He makes an appearance in my Grandpa Wilson's obituary, and I find a West High School alumni page where he lists his occupation as "machine operator." I've seen all of this before, but I do stumble upon something new, a record of a judge denying his request to keep $765 that the state accidentally overpaid him in unemployment benefits.

The only thing that reveals anything about my father's personality is his Flickr account. It's mostly nature shots – hummingbirds, storm clouds, bald eagles – but the very first photograph is of a woman, apparently his girlfriend, lying in bed on her side, wearing high heels and no pants, looking suggestively over her shoulder at the camera with her white thong underwear pulled down low around her hips. This same woman is in the first eight photographs, looking old and dour in some of the shots, but smiling and attractive in others. One of the pictures is a selfie, taken by my father. The woman stands behind him, resting her chin on his shoulder, her face framed by her long blonde hair and bangs. My father has his head pulled back from the camera, trying to get the framing right. He's wearing the sort of cheap, unattractive reading glasses that you can buy off the shelf at the pharmacy for a few bucks, and I'm struck by how much he's aged since the last time I saw him. He's a year away from turning sixty, I believe, and he looks like nothing so much as a skinnier, sicklier version of Papa.

After the adoption was finalized, I agreed to start spending some time with my dad. Alice was livid about it. For years, she'd been telling anyone who would listen that I could see my father whenever I wanted, and that I *chose* not to have anything to do with him. But now that my choice wasn't exactly what she wanted, she opposed it at every turn. She listened in on our phone calls. She tried to limit the time we spent together to an hour, even though my father had to drive a hundred miles to see me.

My dad would pick me up in his beat-up, cigarette-smelling car, and we would drive down gravel roads to state parks, or to the homes of distant relatives, or, if Alice allowed us enough time, to a bowling alley. The outings were stilted and awkward. I never felt comfortable enough to confront my father about all the things he'd done, all the time he'd missed. My dad acted like we were old friends. He bragged about the $800 bar bill he racked up on a Caribbean cruise he took with the company where he was working, and he blasted Nine Inch Nails and Buckcherry from the radio as we sped down the highway to his Uncle Robert's farm in Baxter. We'd spend chilly spring afternoons wandering Robert's fields, looking for Indian arrowheads. My father claimed to have "Cherokee blood," and every so often he'd bend over and fish something out of the dirt and show it to me with pride, but to me, everything he found just looked like an ordinary rock.

Once, my father told a story about him and my mother, and at the end, he said, "That was before she was riding around on a broom." When I just stared at him, he explained the joke, saying that my mother had turned into a witch. I didn't say anything. I didn't feel close enough to tell him what I'd never stopped believing, even as I'd decided to allow him back into my life. I didn't tell him what a piece of shit I still thought he was.

When I moved to Iowa City for college, my father came down to see me a couple of times a semester, driving the same route he'd taken two decades earlier, when he brought my mom to the "home for unwed mothers." The other guys on my floor had sturdy, reliable dads with boring jobs and amiable smiles, dads who would help them build a loft bed for their dorm room and then take them out for a steak. My dad was squirrelly and shifty and small. When he visited, we would just drive around town together, or play Frisbee golf at a state park. By then, he'd moved in with my Grandma Wilson, and he complained constantly about my teenage cousins, how they hogged the computer, how they interrupted the Internet connection while he was trying to illegally download music from Napster. My face grew hot listening to him, but again, I said nothing.

As I got closer to graduation, my patience grew thin. My father had been back in my life for nearly seven years, and still, he hadn't added anything. I didn't like who I became when I was around him – a meek, awkward little boy who just sat there dumbly while he badmouthed my mom and my cousins and entire races of people. During the spring of my senior year, a few months before I was set to move to New York to teach middle school, he forgot my birthday, then emailed me a few days later to complain about his new job at a meatpacking plant, and to tell me that my cousin Wanda was white trash, a lousy mother, and a druggie who was just using my Grandma Wilson.

This time, I didn't hold back. "You call Wanda a bad

mom, but what kind of dad are you?" I wrote, emboldened behind my computer screen. "You say she's using Grandma, but you're still living with your mom, and you're almost fifty. You found a syringe – so what? You've never done any drugs? I'm sick of putting up with your shit."

I went on like this for a while. "Everything I've ever done has been on my own, and I don't owe you anything," I wrote at the end. "I'm moving to New York in June, and I'll be there for two years. If there's anything you want to make good on, you'd better hurry."

What did I expect to come from this? Did I really think that my dad would apologize, that he would weep and ask forgiveness and try to make things right? Did I think that I would suddenly have a real father?

I think a part of me did. It's why I gave him a chance when I was fifteen. It's why my younger brothers both took chances on him years later, long after I'd given up. Like me, they ended up disappointed, relearning what we've known all our lives: that our father is not a man who can be counted on, that he has nothing to offer us. But we had to be sure. We had to see for ourselves.

This was my father's reply:

We have nothing more to say to each other as far as I'm concerned. No, maybe someday we should find out if you are really a Hennick. Your mother was sleeping with someone about the time she got pregnant. Your father may be a tuna fisherman from Florida, ask her. You'll die teaching some spick or nigger in New York from a spike in the chest. How stupid.

After I read the email, I sat numb, staring at the screen. It was eight o'clock on a freezing night in early March, and although I'd just turned twenty-two, I was already trying to quit drinking. With some whiskey, I could have handled this.

I could have nipped at the bottle until the words blurred on the screen and didn't feel so important. But sober, I had no idea how to even begin to process it.

Days later, I would go to a shooting range with a friend, envisioning my father's face as I aimed the assault rifle at the target. I would print the email out and show everybody I knew and watch how they reacted, and then I would try to feel the anger and the outrage that I saw on their faces, instead of the hollowed-out feeling that had taken up residence inside my chest.

But on that night, I opened the front door of my third-floor apartment and let the icy air blast into the living room. The building encircled a pool, which was drained for the winter and covered with black vinyl that sagged under a pile of unmelted snow. Earlier in the year, I'd subscribed to a dozen different news and culture magazines. I thought that, even if I didn't have powerful parents, and even if I didn't attend an Ivy League school, I could still read the same things that people were reading at Harvard and Yale. If I read what they read, I thought, maybe I would learn whatever it was they knew that made them who they were, and who I wasn't. The whole apartment was littered with these magazines, and now the sight of them made me feel babyish and naive, stupid enough to think I could change who I was through a handful of magazine subscriptions.

Next to the door sat a week-old copy of The New Republic. I picked it up and stepped out onto the concrete walkway in just my jeans and tee shirt, too pumped with adrenaline to feel the cold. I cocked my arm back, and then threw the magazine as hard as I could over the railing. It shot out into the night, but then the pages opened up, and the magazine began to flutter, falling softly until it landed on the pool cover below.

"You can't fix me, New Republic!" I shouted into the darkness. "I'm a piece of shit! Don't you know who my father is?"

I picked up a copy of The New Yorker and sent it flying over the railing. "Your cartoons suck, anyway!"

I left the door open and tramped back to my bedroom, gathering a load of Newsweeks and Atlantics, then brought them outside and threw them out onto the covered pool, one by one. "Fuck you!" I shouted after them as they fell. "Go play with your rich friends. Didn't anybody tell you about me? Didn't they tell you that I'm worthless? People have been telling me for years, and I should have fucking listened."

Day 8

I AWAKE AT 5:15 A.M. in Alice's darkened basement. Nile is tossing and turning in the bed, tugging at the covers. "I want to watch that," he whines. "I want to watch that."

I cuddle him close to me and stroke his hair, thinking he's talking in his sleep. "We'll watch it in a little bit," I say, playing along, trying to calm him down.

But then Nile turns to face me, his eyes wide open, and says, "No, I want to watch TV."

"There isn't a TV down here, baby."

Nile points at a shadowy rectangle on the wall. "Then what's that?"

"It's a picture," I tell him. "A picture of Jesus."

Alice was raised Catholic and attended parochial school as a girl, but she'd mostly fallen away from religion by the time I came into her life. I can only remember her bringing me to a Catholic church once, for her great-nephew's confirmation ceremony. I fell into evangelical Christianity after a meeting a born-again yogurt salesman on a flight to Boston to see my mom when I was twelve years old, and I began attending church on my own in Maxwell. I think I was attracted to religion both because it offered a sense that there was order in the universe, and because it offered unconditional love and acceptance. Alice made fun of me mercilessly for the gold cross that dangled from my neck. "Nobody wants a virgin," she used to tell me. "You may be a Bible thumper, but I'll get to heaven before you ever will."

Alice is no more religious now than she was when I lived with her, but she has this one painting in the basement of Christ kneeling and attending to a lost sheep.

"Well," Nile says. "I don't believe in God."

"That's fine, baby," I say. "Go back to sleep."

But he's wide awake now, and he keeps asking for television, and eventually I give in and take him upstairs. Alice and Harry's rooms, directly across from one another at the end of the hall, both have their doors open, and the hallway glows with the sort of staggered blue light that comes from televisions left on in the middle of the night. Nile bounds up into Alice's bed without waiting for an invitation, and the dog goes crazy, circling and sniffing, trying to figure out what's going on. Alice wakes up just enough to make room for Nile in the bed, and then she immediately falls back asleep.

From the living room, a clock chimes out seven bells, but the clock radio on Alice's nightstand reads 3:48. There's at least one clock in every room in the house, but none of them agree with each other.

"Come back downstairs if you need anything," I say to Nile, but already his eyes are glued to the infomercial playing on TV.

The morning drags on forever. I put in a load of laundry and wait for Alice to wake up, but she's still sleeping when it's time for Nile to eat breakfast, and I give him two Nutri-Grain bars and a chocolate milk in bed and take the dog for a walk while he eats.

When Alice finally gets up, I ask her what she wants to do with the day, and she says, "Oh, nothing," and then goes to the backyard to smoke a cigarette and poke at her rhubarb plant. We eventually decide we'll take a trip to Target, where Alice wants to buy Nile a Lego set, but she can't quite seem to get going. I leave Nile with her for just a few minutes while she's supposed to be getting ready, but when I come back upstairs, she's wandering in and out the back door, seemingly forgetting that he's there.

"Come on, baby," I say to him, worried he'll walk off into the street while she isn't watching. "Come downstairs, and I'll show you my baseball cards. Grandma Alice needs to get dressed."

"She's already dressed." Nile points at Alice, who is standing once again pantless in the backyard, wearing the same tattered white tee shirt she had on when we arrived. "She looks pretty in that."

I take Nile to the basement and pull two long, squat Tupperware boxes out from underneath the bed, and then I dismantle The Shrine and open up the blue trunk. In just a few minutes, the floor is strewn with boxes and albums of baseball cards, unopened Starting Lineup figurines, and dozens of newspapers and magazines that I hoarded, thinking, for some ridiculous reason, that people would one day want to purchase the sports section of the Waterloo Courier from the day after Michael Jordan's first retirement from basketball. The Starting Lineup figurines are only worth a couple of dollars each after all these years, and I let Nile open them up and play with them while I check the crawlspace on the unfinished side of the basement. There, in four large Tupperware crates, I find thousands more baseball cards. I leave them where they are, not wanting to make an even bigger mess, but I also spot a shoebox of old photographs, and I carry these with me back to the finished side of the basement, setting them next to my luggage so I'll remember to take them with us when we leave.

After a while, Alice calls down from upstairs to say she's ready to go. On the car ride to Target, she at first refuses to put her seatbelt on, but then the car beeps at her so incessantly that she has no other choice. She keeps forgetting that we're leaving tomorrow, and she tries several times to make plans two or three days out. She gossips crassly about distant family members, telling me about alleged affairs that occurred three decades ago.

When we arrive at Target, Alice insists on letting me use her placard to park in a handicap spot. I feel funny doing it, and would rather just drop her off at the entrance and then park in a regular spot, but I follow her instructions. During the thirty-foot walk to the store, she lights up a cigarette and takes quick, desperate drags from it. "Just a puff," she says. "I just need a puff." Then, as soon as we're inside, she wants to stop at the snack shop for a sandwich.

We've been in Waterloo for less than a day, and already I'm looking forward to leaving. I feel bad about it. Nile is enjoying himself, and Alice has been looking forward to our visit for months. But I feel like we're all wading through quicksand together.

Pushing the shopping cart through the store, Alice comes back to life a bit. She tells Nile he can pick out any Lego set he wants, but I limit him to the small boxes, since we're going to have to travel with whatever he builds. He picks out a volcano truck set (I'm fairly certain that "volcano trucks" aren't an actual thing that exist outside the Lego universe), and Alice tells him to choose a box of Hot Wheels, too, then begins hunting for something for Peanut. She buys Nile a new pair of swimming trunks and a swim shirt, and she insists on buying me a spare phone charger. She gets Peanut a Finding Nemo hoodie. This is the thing that makes her happiest, spending money on the people she loves.

I think back to those Saturdays three decades ago with Papa and Alice, the "Special Days" when we would wander through stores and they would let me pick out a toy. When I remember those times, here is what gets me: Alice and Papa loved me back then in the same way that I love Nile now. They loved me wholly, completely, unconditionally, uncontrollably. It seems impossible, just totally unimaginable, that they could have loved me that much and then gone on to do the things they did. And yet, both things are true. They really did love me that much, and they really did do those things. The thought is both comforting and scary. It's comforting because, no matter what else happens, those good times can never be erased. In a way, those moments go on forever, and are just as real and relevant as the moments that Nile and I are living now. But it's scary because, what the hell happened to that love? And if you can love a child with your entire heart and then go on to betray that love, what does that say about my love for Nile, which, from everything I can tell, is exactly the same, both in kind and degree, as the love that Papa and Alice felt for me when I was his age?

What I want is for Nile to remember the simple things, details so uncomplicated in their pleasures that they'll be impossible to misinterpret later on. The thrill of bringing a new toy home. The feel of my forearms supporting him as I carried him around the Hall of Fame. The sound of my voice reading him a book as he falls asleep. But what if there are more complicated, less happy, times ahead of us? What if those are the days he remembers?

The thought is devastating to me.

• • •

When we get back to the house, Nile exits the car clutching his new toys tight to his chest, as though he's afraid I might try to steal them. I make him a grilled cheese sandwich and some steamed broccoli for lunch, and by the time I've finished preparing the meal, Alice has already gone back to bed.

Harry is in the living room, sitting in his recliner and watching television. For ten straight minutes, a woman on the TV complains about pit bulls, and I realize that he's watching a City Council meeting in its entirety. He must watch twelve or thirteen hours of television each day. Nile finishes his food, and I set him up with his Legos and leave him in the living room with Harry while I go outside to mow the lawn.

After I finish up, I give Nile a bath upstairs, then take my own shower in the basement stall while Nile lies in bed with Alice and re-watches "Charlotte's Web." Drying off, I carefully tiptoe around my baseball cards, which are still scattered on the floor, along with the elements of The Shrine. There's another small wedding portrait on the wall, and my eyes are drawn toward it. I don't have any photographs of Papa up at home, and it's strange to see him again now, everywhere I turn. In this picture, he and Alice are both looking at the camera, each with a hand on Alice's bouquet. Alice looks like an entirely different person, her skin taut, her mouth affixed in a beaming smile, and her long, straight hair pulled back into a bun. But Papa is recognizable as the man I knew growing up, only younger. His dark hair appears almost jet black against the white of his wedding tux. His enormous eyeglasses are only slightly less enormous than the ones he wore later in life, and although his face is less wrinkled, it's already creased with a couple of deep lines. Now that I'm looking closely, I see the same hesitant smile that I noticed in the family portrait yesterday. Maybe I'm just seeing this everywhere, now that I'm looking for it. Or maybe that's just who Papa was, a deeply uncertain man, floating through life, relying on whatever woman he was with at the time to tell him what to do until he grew sick of listening to her and moved on to someone new.

The day Papa told us he was leaving, he'd only been back

from Las Vegas for a few days. It was a Saturday, early in the spring of my sophomore year of high school, and the morning started like any other, with Alice yelling at me for some trivial thing and telling me I couldn't go out with my friends that night. I had a speech competition that day, and it's possible that Alice tried to ban me from that, too. She was constantly doing this sort of thing, threatening to keep me from track practice or the school play as punishment for minor infractions. Once, she grounded me from an athletics banquet where I was supposed to receive an award because a friend had lost a video game I'd lent him.

I was glad to get out of the chaos of the house and into the nerdy calm of the speech competition, where I recited Poe's "The Raven" in a monotone and received a middling score. The competition was out of town, and it was early evening by the time I got home.

The moment I walked into the house, I knew something was wrong. In the morning, Alice had been a tornado, hurling insults and accusations at me as quickly as she could think of them, but now, the house was oddly still. The lights in the kitchen were off, and Alice and Papa were sitting in silence in the living room, Papa in his recliner and Alice on the couch. They both stared at the blank screen of the turned-off television.

"Calvin," Alice said, her voice catching. "Come in here. Your grandfather has something he needs to tell you."

Immediately, I thought they were kicking me out of the house. Alice had been telling me for years that all she had to do was get Papa to agree to it, and I would be out on the street.

Haltingly, I stepped into the living room. I could hear the ticking of a clock. I could hear the high-pitched whine of a brass lamp.

"In Las Vegas," Papa began, and then cleared his throat. "I met someone."

"A younger woman," Alice said, her voice full of spite.

"She's not either," Papa said.

Alice stared daggers into him. "She's eighteen years younger than you are."

"So what?" Papa said. "You're eleven years younger than I am."

"Like I said," Alice sneered. "A younger woman."

It was clear that they'd been having some version of this same fight for hours. I realized I was still standing up, still holding onto my backpack. I set it on the floor and walked across the room to the only remaining chair. I looked from Papa to Alice and back again, but neither of them looked at me. Papa kept staring at the television screen, trying not to meet anyone's eyes. Alice never took her eyes off of Papa.

"So," Papa said. "I'm going back to Las Vegas. To live with Marie."

"My God!" Alice said, rolling her eyes up to the ceiling. "Do you have to call her that?"

"What?" Papa said. "Marie? That's her name. What do you want me to call her?"

"How about your goddamned whore? How about that?"

I rubbed at my eyes, as though I might be dreaming all of this. It felt surreal. In the past, Papa and Alice had had fights where they threw the word "divorce" around. They would yell at each other, and Papa would say that he wanted a divorce. Alice would say he could have one just as soon as he signed over half of everything he owned, and Papa would say he'd be goddamned if he was going to give her half the house and half his money after all she'd already spent. Whenever they had those fights, I would hold my breath, trying not to let on what I was secretly thinking, that I hoped it would be for real this time; that I hoped Papa would finally get so fed up with Alice that he would give her whatever she wanted to make her go away. But then, a day would pass, and everything would be normal again.

Now it was real, but Papa wasn't kicking Alice out. He was leaving.

"What about me?" I said. Alice and Papa both looked up, as though just now remembering that I was in the room. "What's going to happen to me?"

"You can come and live with Marie and me in Las Vegas, and I'll sell the house," Papa said. "Or, you can stay here in the house. With Alice."

I didn't want either of those things. I didn't want to move to Las Vegas, to leave behind the friends I'd finally made. I didn't want to start over in the middle of high school someplace where I wouldn't know anybody, someplace where my credits might not transfer, someplace where there would be ten times as many students as there were in Maxwell. And I definitely didn't want to be left alone with Alice for the next three years. But more than any of this, I didn't want to be given the *choice* between those two things. I didn't want the responsibility of deciding whether Alice would have to leave.

I didn't say any of this. Instead, I said, "You're leaving."

"Hey," Papa said, finally looking me in the eye. "I'm not just running out the door."

His voice sounded almost wounded. He repeated the bit about how I could stay in the house if I wanted, or I could come with him. Either way, he said, he would continue paying for my health insurance. As though that was what I cared about right now.

"You're leaving," I said again.

"I'm taking responsibility here," Papa said. "I'm not abandoning you."

I got up and walked out the door. That morning, Alice had told me I was grounded, but I didn't care now. I needed to get out of the house. What could she do to me at this point, anyway? My rusted burgundy Buick sat in the driveway, and I got behind the wheel and drove in silence to a restaurant in another town, where my friends were meeting for pizza. Halfway through dinner, I mentioned that my grandparents were getting divorced. My friends didn't believe me at first, and then, once they realized I was serious, things were awkward. After dinner, I walked around the town by myself, stuffing my hands into the pockets of my spring jacket to keep warm, trying to kill enough time that Papa and Alice would be asleep when I got home.

When I walked inside, the house was dark and quiet. Papa and Alice had slept in separate bedrooms since I'd been living with them, and now Papa was asleep in his room on the first floor, and Alice was upstairs in her bedroom, which, for some reason, had two king beds in it. There was a note on the kitchen counter.

Calvin,
You can come sleep upstairs, if you want to.
Love,
Granny

I didn't know what to make of this. I'd never called Alice "Granny," not once in my entire life. Was she trying to form an alliance with me? Was she trying to convince me to stay here with her in Maxwell? Was she simply lonely and wanted company? Or did she really think, somehow, that I would want to be with her right now?

Grudgingly, I grabbed the pillow from my own bed and trudged upstairs. I felt a sense of obligation, or maybe guilt. I felt that, if I didn't join Alice, I would be betraying her somehow.

Alice lay on her back, motionless, in the bed nearest to the door. I took the other bed, lying on top of the covers, still wearing my slacks and dress shirt from the speech competition.

"You awake?" I asked, looking up at the dark ceiling.

"Yep."

"So what's going to happen?"

"You heard him," Alice said. Her voice sounding more tired now than angry. "He's going to Las Vegas to be with his girlfriend."

I didn't say anything, and a long moment stretched out in the dark silence. "You know what I asked him?" Alice finally said. "I asked him, does he want to leave because I'm so terrible? Or does he want to leave because this other woman is so fabulous? And do you know what he said to me? 'Both.' He said 'both.' He's not going to change his mind."

"But what happens with us?" I said. "I mean, you and me."

"Calvin," Alice said. "That's entirely up to you."

In fact, it wasn't up to me at all. I was too timid to bring the issue up again, and somehow, it was decided for me: I would be staying here in Maxwell with Alice. In three days, Papa was gone.

• • •

Five minutes away from Chuck E. Cheese, Nile falls asleep in the back of the Black Racer. "Christ," I mutter. "Now he's going to be a terror." I glance at the clock. "And we're going to be late." It took Alice an hour and a half to get ready, and she looks like a whole new person in her black-and-white watercolor tunic and pressed white capri pants. A long gold chain dangles from her neck.

"Do you know how many times I've had to wait for those two?" Alice says. "Screw 'em!" After a moment, she adds, "I think that's funny, what Nile said about not being able to go to Willy's house because of your dad."

"Don't bring it up," I tell her.

"Oh, I won't. But he needs to know." Alice takes her cigarettes out of her purse. "Now, I need just a puff before we go in there. Just a taste."

"Not in the car."

The strip mall with the Chuck E. Cheese comes into view, and I pull into the parking lot. My Grandma Wilson and Aunt Jane are standing out front. Grandma Wilson is wearing a pastel green polo shirt, khaki pants, and practical white sneakers, and her short, curled hair has been colored a pale yellow. Jane is bigger than the last time I saw her. She wears a teal top and the short up-do hairstyle of Midwestern middle age, and it only now occurs to me that she's sixty years old. I'm 34, with two kids, but I still haven't fully gotten used to the idea that I'm an adult, that I'm roughly the same age as my aunts and uncles all were when I was Nile's age, and that they're now the same age that my grandparents were back then.

I tap on my horn and wave to Grandma Wilson and Jane, then pull the car into a spot and set the parking brake.

"Did you fart?" Alice says, hearing the scrunching sound of the brake. "Shit your pants?"

"No." I get out of the car and hug Grandma Wilson and Jane, then return to the Black Racer to help Alice out of her seat. "Nile fell asleep," I call out. "Go inside into the air conditioning, and we'll be in in a minute."

Alice follows them into the arcade, and I open Nile's car door and whisper him awake. "Hey, baby," I say, unbuckling him. "Come here. You still tired? Come here, baby. Careful."

I think I'm going to have to pick Nile up and carry him, but he climbs out of the car by himself and stands there for a moment, looking stunned and sleepy. Then he takes my hand, and we walk inside.

Everybody is still standing at the front, waiting to get their hands stamped so that the staff can check later and make sure that they're not leaving with someone else's child. "Well, hello!" Grandma Wilson says, seeing Nile. "I'm your Grandma Wilson!"

Nile presses his face into my belly. He's met Grandma Wilson – who is, without exaggeration, the sweetest, gentlest person I've ever known – once before, but he's in no mood for reintroductions.

I place my hand on his back and make him stand up straight. "Can you say, 'Hi, Grandma Wilson'?"

Nile sleep-says it, the words all stretched out. "Hiiiiii, Grandmaaaaa Willlllllssssson."

"I'm so glad to see you!" she says.

We find seats and try to figure out the different meal-and-token deals. As soon as we've selected one, Nile takes the token cup and leads Grandma Wilson around to the different games, suddenly fully awake. They sit together in the blue cockpit of a racing game, driving around a virtual track together.

This is the same location, Jane tells me, where we used to have birthday parties when I was a little boy. Back then, it was called ShowBiz Pizza Place, and the chief mascot was Billy Bob, an animatronic, guitar-playing bear. There used to be an enormous ball pit, but that's been replaced by a ladders-and-tunnels play structure, for safety reasons, I assume. I can remember diving under the colorful plastic balls, and then other kids would jump off the sides of the pit and land on my ribs.

Alice's widowed sister and her new husband stop by to say hi, along with one of Alice's nieces and her kids. Jane's husband Ron stops by, too. It's like a little family reunion, even though Nile, Grandma Wilson, and Jane are the only ones related to me by blood.

Nile comes over to me, panting and excited to climb in the play structure. I hold his shoes for him and let him loose, but when he gets to the top, he starts shouting at all the other kids to calm down. "Daddy?" he shouts, banging on the clear plastic window of a pretend police car. "Can you come up here?"

My mind flashes back to the way I used to stand at the top of the stairs at bedtime when I was eight years old, yelling at everybody else to be quiet. It's strange, the things you pass on to your kids.

"I'm not allowed," I call back up to him.

Nile throws his hands the air. "But a bunch of children up here are way too loud and way too fast!"

• • •

After we eat, Nile runs off with Grandma Wilson again. Alice sits chatting with her family in another booth, and Ron goes home, leaving just Jane and me to talk. I tell her that I'm planning to visit Papa's grave for the first time when Nile and I get to Maxwell.

"That's still a sore spot," Jane says. And then I remember: Alice wanted to go to the burial service, but my father told her she couldn't. "Your dad didn't ... he was as diplomatic as he could be. But we had to share Papa his whole life. First with Alice, and then after he went out to Las Vegas. He was always somebody's husband. We needed him to be our dad again."

"Jane," I say, smiling. "You don't have to explain your-self. I am familiar with the complicated feelings that come with being the child of a difficult father."

Jane laughs. She's good-natured and compassionate, and now that Grandma Wilson is getting older, she's become sort of the matriarch on this side of the family, managing my grandmother's finances and arranging her doctor's appointments. Somehow, she's also become one of the only people I can really talk to about my father and my grandfather. Alice doesn't carry on conversations about them so much as she spouts off catchphrases: *Your grandfather had us all fooled, didn't he? Your father just makes me want to puke!* And although I'm close with my mom, she seems to take it personally whenever I mention anything bad about the past, as though I'm holding her responsible for everything that's ever gone wrong. But Jane just listens.

"I see a lot of my dad in your dad," Jane says, and it takes me a beat to remember that her dad is Papa. "When I was young, I had to sit down and grieve the things that I knew were never going to happen. I wrote letters that I never sent, where I said how I wished things were this way or that way. But after a while, I stopped expecting my dad to change. And then, if he gave me a little something more than I was expecting, that was a bonus. I loved him, but he was who he was."

I don't know all of the details or the timeline of Papa's divorce from Grandma Wilson, but I imagine he must have disappointed Jane and my father and their brother Luke in all the same ways he disappointed me. I don't know whether there were big fights, or long periods of silence, but ultimately, it doesn't really matter. After all this time, it's not the details that are important. It's the feelings people are left with.

"What about my dad?" I ask. "What's he up to these days?"

I try to toss out the question casually, not wanting to sound too eager for the information. Not only do I not speak to my father, but I generally don't even speak to anybody *about* my father. Sometimes I'll go a year or more without hearing any sort of update. I know that he still lives in my grandmother's basement, and that he was diagnosed with COPD a while back, but that's it. I don't know if he's working. I don't know if he's still with the girlfriend from the Flickr photos. I don't know anything.

"He's in a sad place," Jane says. "And he made those choices himself, but now he has that lung problem, and his health isn't good enough to hold down a job. He helps out with Grandma, and that gives me peace of mind, even though I know that living there just about drives him crazy."

"Drives *him* crazy? Jane, he's sixty years old." I can feel the old anger rising up – the quickening of my pulse, the shot of adrenaline turning my palms wet and my legs rubbery. "If he doesn't like it, he can get his own fucking place." I put my hand up and apologize for the language.

"No, but he can't," Jane says. Her voice is kind, not defensive. "He can't work. He can't breathe half the time. But it's not bad enough that he can get on disability, and sometimes I think he keeps smoking just so it does get bad enough."

I nod. That sounds like him. Looking for a way to get rewarded for smoking himself to death.

"Here's what I can't understand," I say. "My dad has three sons, and none of them speak with him. Papa ran away to Las Vegas, and then he wondered why we all didn't kiss his ass. Didn't it ever occur to them that any of this might be their fault? Especially now that I'm a father, I just can't imagine blaming my kids for my own problems."

"They're missing something," Jane says. "The connection

piece that the rest of us have, that just didn't come through, somehow. I think they're limited, in a way. I don't know if it's by choice, or if it's the way they were born. I don't know if either of them were ever capable of anything more."

I say nothing. I know what it's like to have flaws that you don't feel like you can fix. But I don't know what it's like not to try.

. . .

At the end of the night, Nile trades in his handful of prize tickets for some Tootsie Rolls, and we all walk out together to the parking lot to say our goodbyes. It's not quite dusk, but gray clouds cover the parking lot, blanketlike and seemingly very low in the sky, and in the distance, I can see just a strip of blue between the horizon and the cloud cover. I've noticed this since we entered Iowa, the way the clouds seem to sit just barely above the treetops, and I wonder whether it's a real meteorological phenomenon, or if it's just an optical illusion, something related to the sheer amount of sky you're able to see when everything is so flat.

Grandma Wilson and Jane each give Nile a small Lego set from Jane's car, his second and third sets of the day. Nile gives them reluctant hugs, not wanting to say goodbye.

"Oooooh," he moans as I buckle him into the Black Racer. "Can I put the Legos together tonight?"

"You can put one of them together in the morning," I say. "Before we leave for Maxwell."

"You're ruining my life," Nile says, but his heart isn't in it. He's too tired to be really angry.

I shut his door and get into the driver's seat. "Yeah, yeah."

"I was talking to Willy," Alice says, as I pull the Black Racer out of the lot. "Watching Nile, you can really see what your father has been missing out on all these years. But then, Papa did the same thing. It's funny how we get along now – Willy and me, I mean. She said, 'You know, I used to hate you.' And I said, 'Big deal!' We have so much fun, the times when we've come out to Boston together. We sit and talk on the plane, and as soon as one of us asks a question, we both forget what we're talking about. It's just ridiculous!"

This isn't something I'd considered before the trip, but the more I think about my family, the more mysterious these dynamics seem. Alice and Grandma Wilson hated each other, but now they're friends. Papa loved Grandma Wilson and stopped, then loved Alice and stopped, and then loved Marie. Alice loved me, then hated me, then loved me again. Papa loved me and then left. Alice has always hated my father and still hates him. There's no rational way to account for this, how some of the feelings have changed over time, and others have stubbornly refused to budge.

When we get to the house, Nile wants to sleep upstairs with Alice, but I know that the TV will be on all night, and the dog will be jumping all over him. If I let him have his way tonight, he'll be throwing bleary-eyed tantrums in Maxwell tomorrow.

"You can come up here when you wake up in the morning," Alice tells him.

"I'll be fine," Nile says. "I'll be fine, Daddy. Okay? I'll be fine."

I crouch down to get to his eye level. "Listen to me. I need you to get a good night's sleep with me downstairs."

He relents, grumbling, and we go down to the basement and do our bedtime routine in the big bed. "I need you to sleep with me," Nile says in a demanding little voice. "If you want me to close my eyes, you have to sleep with me the whole night."

"I'll lie down until you fall asleep," I tell him. "But then I need to clean up these baseball cards." The floor is still littered with them.

Nile drifts off to sleep almost immediately. I know I'm pushing him to his limits on this trip, but he's having fun. For months after we get back to Boston, he'll talk about Iowa at bedtime each night, asking when we can come back.

I get out of bed and start scooping up the baseball cards, being careful with the edges, even though I know they're not worth anything now. The cards that make me the happiest aren't the glossy, foil-stamped ones that I collected in my early teens, but the drab, off-center ones from the late eighties and early nineties. I remember opening up the wax packages, the joy of discovering a Mark McGwire or a Jose Canseco card, back before those heroes fell to injuries and scandal. I remember Papa sitting at a table with the cards all spread out in front of him, the tip of his tongue stuck out in concentration as he showed me how to alphabetize them, and I smile.

But the happy memory is just a flash, instantly replaced by everything that came later. After Papa left, I thought that things with Alice might get better, now that I was all she had. But things only got worse. She blamed me for Papa leaving, even though they were already living apart for half the year when I arrived. "If it weren't for you," she'd snarl at me, "I'd be out in Las Vegas with my husband, where I belong." One night, I waited until she was asleep, then packed my clunky Buick up with everything that would fit and drove out to my friend Brett's house. His parents had told me once that I could come out and stay with them anytime I needed to, but looking back, I'm sure they were surprised when I actually showed up. Alice had been threatening for years to kick me out of the house, and I didn't think she would care that much that I'd left, but I was wrong. She demanded that I come home. I'd bought the Buick with my own savings, but it was registered in her name, and she threatened to phone the police and report it stolen. I called Papa for help, but he didn't want to deal with it. "You left me alone with her," I told him. "You knew what she was like, and you left me alone with her."

"Hey," Papa said. "I don't have to listen to this."

"You don't have to listen if you don't want to," I said. "But I have some things to say, and I'm going to say them."

Papa hung up.

Dejected, I drove back to the house and unpacked my car. Nothing changed with Alice until I left for college, and I talked to Papa only occasionally after that. Twice during college, I went to Las Vegas to see him, but I never felt close to him again. The last time I saw him in person was nearly seven years before he died, when Belzie and I went to Vegas for a brief vacation. He and his girlfriend Marie took us out to a buffet to eat, and then we played blackjack for a little while.

As time went on, I found it more difficult to find things to talk about on the phone. We'd commiserate about the fortunes of the Iowa Hawkeyes for a little while, and then I'd try to talk to him about gambling. For someone who'd lived in Las Vegas for years, he had a glaring lack of basic knowledge about probabilities, but I went along with him, bullshiting about how you could get a deck of cards working in your "favor" during a game of blackjack, how the two card is the "dealer's ace." After a while, we'd run out of things to say, and whole minutes would pass in silence before one of us said he had to go.

Once Nile was born, I stopped making much of an effort. I was busy, and Papa didn't call very often, and it felt like a better use of my time to read a book to my baby boy than to sit on the phone in awkward silence with my distant grandfather. Months went by without any contact, and I thought that maybe we were done with each other. But when his birthday came around, I called him out of a sense of obligation, and I discovered that it felt good to hear his voice again. I fantasized about making it out to Las Vegas one last time and introducing Papa to my son. At Christmastime, I made sure to send him a card, with a picture of Nile tucked inside. Nile was eighteen months old, and in the photo he was sitting on Santa's lap, smiling with his entire face, like life was just the best fucking thing ever.

Then, on Christmas Eve, Papa called. Belzie and I had company over, and so I let it go to voicemail and planned to call Papa back the next day. When I listened to the message on Christmas morning, though, I discovered that he hadn't called to wish me a happy holiday. He'd called to complain that I hadn't included Marie's name on the card. "We're very upset," he said on the message. "We want to know the meaning of this."

I felt deflated. Papa had been gone for years, but he had managed to ruin Christmas from across the country. I didn't want to do this anymore, didn't want to give him or anybody else the power to keep hurting me. Instead of returning the call, I sent him a letter. I explained that I hadn't meant to leave Marie's name off the card, but that I couldn't believe he would call me on Christmas to bawl me out over what was essentially a clerical error. From now on, I told him, I'd just do what he'd been doing for years. I wouldn't send any cards at all.

I didn't hear back from him, and I didn't spend much time worrying about it. I went sledding with Nile. I chased him on the playground and drove him to touch-the-truck days at fire stations. For his second birthday, Alice and Grandma Wilson came out to Boston, and we all stayed up late together the night before his party, trying to get the frosting for the cake fire truck red. The people who wanted to be in my life were in it, and the people who didn't, weren't. It was better this way.

I look around the basement at the photos of Papa, staring out at me from behind his thick eyeglasses. I think about what Jane said, how she needed to grieve the person she wanted him to be, and how she figured out a way to accept him for who he was.

There's a desk and a rickety chair against the wall, across from the bed, and I go to my bag and take out a legal pad and a pen. The baseball cards can wait. I sit down and open the pad up to a clean page, and I write a letter to my dead grandfather.

Day 9

ALICE COMES OUT TO THE DRIVEWAY to see us off, standing in front of the house in only her patterned silk nightgown and brown slippers. Her arms and shoulders are completely bare, and her neckline plunges down to reveal the cleavage of her sagging bosom. She puffs away on a Pall Mall while I load up, and Nile paces around the Black Racer, not meeting Alice's eyes, unable to handle the emotion of the impending good-bye. Alice gets a little weepy, too, as I lift the last bag into the trunk. I know she wishes we were staying longer.

"Come on, Nile," I say. "Let me get a picture of you with Grandma Alice."

Alice drops her cigarette on the driveway and stubs it out with the heel of her slipper, and Nile goes and stands next to her, but he won't look up for the picture. He tucks his chin into his chest and squirms his shoulders.

"Fine," I say, lowering my phone. "Just give Grandma Alice a hug."

Nile presses his face into Alice's silk nightgown, and she wraps her arms around him in a limp bear hug. "I love you," she says.

"I love you, too," Nile says.

"I'll come and see you," Alice says. "Grandma Wilson and I will come out to see you next summer."

This is the fourth or fifth time she's mentioned this, and although I know it's never going to happen, I've only gently pushed back against the idea. Jane has told me that Grandma

Wilson can't travel anymore, and I'd rather make the trip back out here than host Alice again. But I let her have her fun imagining it.

Alice sniffles as I open Nile's car door for him to get in. Like Nile, she's never been good with goodbyes. She bawled at my high school graduation, and again when she dropped me off at college, even though she hated my guts. At the time, it felt almost showy, so disconnected from my day-to-day experiences with her. But now I wonder if there was something else behind it, if she was feeling things more deeply and complexly than I was able to understand.

After Nile is buckled in, Alice bends down into the car, getting in one last goodbye. "When your daddy was a little boy," she tells him, "we'd say, 'I love you THIS MUCH!'" She opens her arms as wide as they'll go, spreading them out in front of Nile's face. "Look. I love you THIS MUCH!"

"I love you so much, too," Nile says.

Alice gives him a final hug, and I shut Nile into the car.

"Oh, God," Alice says, pulling me into a weak embrace.

"We'll see you soon," I say.

"Okay," Alice says. "I love you."

"I love you, too, Alice."

She lights up another Pall Mall, and I walk around to get into the Black Racer and begin to back out of the driveway. Alice stands in front of the garage in her nightgown, smoking and watching us leave.

The next time I talk to Alice, after Nile and I are back in Boston, she will tell me that she went to bed for four days after our visit, barely even getting up to eat or use the bathroom. In the following weeks, she'll grow more depressed, talking often about how she's ready to die. And then, sometime around Thanksgiving, something will change. When I call, she'll have difficulty carrying on a conversation. She'll begin falling, sometimes lying on the floor for hours before her brother discovers her and helps her up. Her worried nieces will take her to the doctor, who will order an MRI, and the test will reveal brain shrinkage and blood vessel damage. She will be diagnosed with dementia, and although the doctors won't be able to say for sure what's caused the sudden slide, they'll all agree that she will never be the same. Less than a year from today, she will be moved into a nursing home.

If I'd known that this would be the last time I'd see Alice – the real Alice – would I have done anything differently? Are there things I would have said, things I would have asked? The cliché is that you should tell people how you feel about them now, because one day it will be too late. But what if there aren't any words for how you feel? What if the only way to describe it is to just start at the beginning and say every single thing that has ever happened between the two of you?

Never mind the feelings. I don't even have the language to talk about the way the people in my family are related to me. This woman in the driveway, giving me a final wave goodbye with her cigarette hand before I disappear down the road, is my father's father's second ex-wife. But she is also the person who loved me as a boy, who hated me as a teenager, who, for better or worse, stayed with me when everybody else had left. And, according to Iowa adoption records, she is my mother.

There's no word for all of this. And so I have my own word: Alice. She's just Alice. Whatever she is, she's mine, and when her brain betrays her and robs her of her personality, I'll miss this crass, unapologetic version of her more than I can know now.

Just as "Alice" is a shorthand to describe a woman whose relationship to me is indescribable, we all have a shared shorthand to talk about our messy, complicated feelings. The words are all but meaningless by themselves, but they're useful as a stand-in for all the things we otherwise wouldn't know how to say. I used this shorthand myself just before I got into the car, and I won't have any regrets about not telling Alice how I feel, because I did tell her, the best that I was able. Two decades ago, when I said them inside a family lawyer's office, the words were a lie, but since then, they've somehow become true.

I told Alice, "I love you."

• • •

Driving through Iowa, the only variation is the sound under the tires. There's the smooth hum of new asphalt, the high-pitched whine of concrete bridges, the *thump, pause, thump, pause* where the road has been patched over. The landscape itself never changes. It's all corn and soybeans, punctuated by the occasional farmhouse surrounded by a grove of trees and a couple of grain silos. Out on these rural highways, the whole state seems to offer itself up to you, as though to say, *This is what we've got, there aren't any secrets here.*

We travel for a while on Route 20, and then turn south onto Highway 65, our first two-lane, undivided highway of the trip. The semi trucks whoosh past us in the opposite direction, and I grip the wheel more tightly, afraid we'll be blown off the road. I point out little rural landmarks to Nile. "There's a sod farm, where they grow grass and sell it to people for their yards," I say. "Over there, that's a grain elevator."

"Oh," Nile says. "Does it go up and down like a person elevator?"

"I actually don't know, baby," I confess. "I lived in Iowa for twenty years, and I have no idea how a grain elevator works."

As Waterloo recedes behind us, I think about what – or, rather, who – we've left behind. It's not lost on me how anticlimactic, absurd almost, it is to travel all this way, thinking about how to be a better man and father, only to get within a mile of my own dad and then leave him in the rearview mirror. If this road trip were a movie, there'd be no getting out of it without an in-the-flesh confrontation. Even if I wanted to escape him, my father would simply show up somewhere. Maybe at Old Settlers, maybe at Papa's grave, maybe at the airport, just as we were about to fly home to Boston. We would have our heart-to-heart, our catharsis, our cautious-but-necessary (for the plot, anyways) reconciliation. If this were a movie, my father would meet Nile, and he'd see the bond I have with my son, and he'd mournfully realize all he'd missed out on. He wouldn't be able to make up for lost time, but he would recognize his failure as a father, and he would say, "I'm sorry." And for the movie version of me, that would be enough.

Life isn't a movie. Our lives don't follow some satisfying dramatic arc. And yet, I know that Belzie is right. Even if I don't see my father, I know I can't leave Iowa without grappling with him somehow. I need to at least try to understand him. And then I need to try to leave him behind.

For lunch, Nile and I stop at a Casey's convenience store that sits right on the side of the highway. The faux red-brick awning of the Iowa-based gas station chain inspires in me a ridiculous wave of nostalgia.

"Smell that?" I say to Nile, helping him out of the car. "Breathe in through your nose."

Nile takes a big whiff. "Yeah."

"What's that smell?" I ask.

"Horses?"

"Nope," I say. "It's pig poop."

"Pig poop?" Nile scrunches up his face. "Ugh! Yuck."

I laugh and take him inside the store. "It's okay, baby. Everything is fine."

Now I feel even more ridiculously nostalgic, the smell of pig shit making me homesick for a place that isn't even my home anymore. Generally, people in Iowa try not to live near a hog confinement if they can help it, but no one really objects to driving through the smell. Out-of-state journalists, when they parachute in for the presidential caucuses every four years, claim that Iowans call the smell of hog manure "the smell of money," but I've never heard anyone actually say this in real life.

Inside Casey's, I get a slice of bacon pizza for myself and a slice of pepperoni for Nile, and then we come back outside to eat at a rickety picnic table behind the store. As soon as we sit down, a gust of prairie wind sends our napkins flying in a little tornado of brown paper. I make a perfunctory, half-hearted attempt to gather them up, but they scatter more quickly than I can chase them. The picnic table is on the edge of a soybean field, and the wind sends ripples through the leaves, so that the field appears to be roiling with green waves.

"AGGHHH!" Nile says.

"What?" I say, thinking he's hurt himself on the table somehow. "What?!"

"A bug landed on my pizza!"

I wave my hand over his slice. "Shake it off," I tell him. "We're in Iowa. The air is full of bugs and pollen and humidity and pig poop. You've got to toughen up."

• • •

We arrive in Maxwell in midday, and I take a lap around town in the Black Racer with Nile before heading out into the country to my friend Brice's parents' house. Cresting the hill into town, we're greeted by a pair of squat, white houses. A sign on the side of the road displays a silhouette of a horse and carriage, along with the words, "Welcome to Maxwell. Home of Old Settlers Picnic and Historical Museum."

"Here we are," I tell Nile. "We made it. This is the town where Daddy's from."

Nile repeats the words in a whisper so low and reverent that it sounds almost mocking. "The town where Daddy's from."

There's a used car for sale on the lawn of the doublewide trailer where my friend Sunday used to live, and a teenage girl is mowing the lawn in shorts and a tank top. In a couple of blocks, we take a left and drive past the high school. It's been renovated several times, but the core building is the same box of dirty red bricks where I learned twenty years ago, and where Papa learned fifty years before that.

"Did you get to ride on one of those?" Nile asks, pointing to the open bus garage on the other side of the street.

"I did."

"Wow." He says this as though I've just told him I'd flown to the moon. "Was it a fun ride?"

"Not really," I say. "The other children were pretty mean to me."

"Oh, like they said, 'Nya nya nya!'" Nile offers. "Like that?"

"No." My mind flashes back to the bus rides I took for four years to and from the middle school in Collins. There weren't any bus monitors, and the drivers didn't care what was happening behind them, as long as everybody was still breathing when they got where they were going. "They would all gang up and push me against the window until I couldn't breathe."

"That's not nice," Nile says.

"People aren't nice sometimes."

Looking back, it's difficult to tell which of my negative experiences were Maxwell's fault, and which were the result of my own bad attitude. Maxwell is bursting with salt-of-the-earth types who would stop to help a stranger change a flat tire in the rain, but it also has plenty of people like A.J. Bird, who threatened to kick my ass for criticizing his decision to fly a giant Confederate flag from the back of his pickup truck. (Iowa was a Union state.) People were *constantly* threatening to kick my ass. Probably, that's a universal high-school thing, but I also had a reputation for being a mouthy know-it-all. I was a pacifist (an extremely convenient thing for a 140-pound weakling with zero fighting skills to be), and I never even pretended that I might be able to hold my own in a fight. When someone threatened to kick my ass, I would tell him he could go ahead, and if he did, I would call the cops. The guy would then usually call me a "pussy," and I would say, no, I would be a "pussy" if I challenged him to a fight and ran crying to the cops after I lost, but since, in fact, I had no interest in fighting, beating my ass would constitute battery, which was a crime, and in this country people weren't allowed to hand out ass-beatings to people they disagree with. At this point, generally, people got sick of listening to me and walked away.

We take a turn and drive for four more blocks, and already we're at the other end of town. My friend Tylor's house, where his parents still live, has Maxwell's "Yard of the Month" sign sticking out of the front lawn. Then we take a left, and we're at the town park. Stan the Junk Man's house used to sit across from it, but it was bulldozed long ago, and now it's just a grassy patch of land owned by the town. A dirt road encircles the park, and Nile and I make a loop, driving the Black Racer past the penned-up rodeo horses and the carnival workers setting up the rides for later. The only activity happening right now is the volleyball tournament, but already a few dozen cars are parked along the grass.

"Look, Daddy," Nile says, pointing. "It's the hot guys."

I look and see that someone has set up a black tailgating tent with the University of Iowa Tigerhawk logo emblazoned on it. "Hawkeyes," I say. "Not 'hot guys.'"

We hit Main Street, where the tiny old car dealership has become a tiny new chiropractor's office. We pass the American Legion, the post office, and the volunteer fire station. We pass the Maxwell Community Center, derided when it was built as the "Taj Mahal" for the tax increase it brought. There's a small grocery store, and a Casey's, and a bar that used to be a video store. I see a few teenagers walking around, the boys in muscle shirts and the girls in short shorts, and for a moment I expect to recognize them, forgetting that I'm twice their age and haven't lived here since before they were born.

The houses are modest – downright tiny, in some cases – but well-maintained, and the yards are huge and lush, with enormous oaks and maples bursting up out of the ground. I'm struck by how little has changed. There's a new water tower, and a small subdivision on the edge of town, but for the most part things are identical to the way they were when I lived here. It's like stepping back in time.

I drive onto Baldwin Street and pull the Black Racer up in front of my old house. It's still white with black shutters, but I can't see much behind the trees and the unpainted picket fence that has been installed in the front yard. Alice used to complain about how the new owners were keeping up the property after she and Papa sold it, as though she still had some sort of claim over the house. But it's changed hands several times since then and appears to be in decent shape. I've looked it up online, and the current owner bought it at a foreclosure auction five years ago, paying less than a tenth of what Belzie and I paid for our house in the Boston suburbs.

I tell Nile that this is where I used to live. Even as sweet and sentimental as he is, this information bores him in the way that every kid in history has been bored looking at the front of the nondescript house where their parents grew up. I'm transfixed, though. I have to fight the urge to get out of the car and knock on the door and ask the owner if I can walk the property. I want to see if the bees still buzz around the pear tree behind the garage. I want to see if the giant walnut tree by the back fence is still littering the yard with its bounty. I wasn't happy when I lived here, and I wanted nothing more than to leave. This is the house where I sat and listened to my grandfather tell me that he was moving to Las Vegas. This is where Alice tried to claw the skin off my arms and made me cry for sport.

I'm so much happier now. And yet, in this moment, all I want to do is wallow in the past.

• • •

Following Brice's directions, I drive along the highway until I see two grain silos, and then I turn left onto a gravel road.

"Did a gravel truck come and dump all this gravel out on the road?" Nile asks, his voice turned into a vibrato from the bumpy surface.

"Probably," I tell him. "And then a steam roller probably came and smoothed it all out."

When I was in high school, I ran on the gravel roads around town to train for track and cross country season, making six- and eight-mile loops on the rural routes surrounding Maxwell. For an hour or more, I would be alone with my thoughts, hearing nothing but the sounds of my own breathing and the *crunch-crunch-crunch* of gravel underneath my shoes. In the summer, I ran at night to avoid the oppressive Iowa heat, carrying a flashlight to shine at passing cars so they wouldn't hit me. When my tee shirt soaked through, I would take it off and tuck it into my shorts, and by the time I got home, my chest would be covered in little black spots – gnats that had flown into me and drowned in my sweat. In the winter, I ran after school, trying to catch the last of the daylight, the freezing air chapping my face and crystallizing in my nostrils.

I take it easy with the Black Racer. The gravel roads in Iowa are crowned, sloping slightly away from the center and down toward the ditches. Most people drive straight down the middle. This helps keep the car from catching the edge of the road and sliding into the ditch, but it also puts you at risk of plowing head-on into another car coming over a hill.

The most dangerous places on gravel roads are the intersections, almost all of which are unregulated. Technically, the right-of-way belongs to the driver on the right, but in practice, it's impossible to see another vehicle until you've crashed into it, especially when the corn is six feet high. My high-school classmate Jake was killed in this way last summer, just after Old Settlers. He was the first of our graduating class to die, and he left five small children behind. Immediately, the town came together to support his family, donating money and bringing meals and coming out to his farm to fix fences and build a new barn. It was terrible, but it made me appreciate the advantages of living and dying in "that same small town," as the song says. If I died in Boston, a couple of our neighbors might check in on Belzie once or twice, and her coworkers might help out with the kids for a bit, but after that, she'd be on her own. "If I die," I told her, only half joking, "you have to move to Maxwell."

Driving out to Brice's parents' house, we pass by a cow pasture, a windmill, and a couple of farmhouses. There's an unmarked intersection and a couple of small hills, and I approach each with what is probably a comical level of caution. And then a property with two camper trailers in the yard comes into view, and I can make out the figure of Brice's dad on his riding lawnmower. Until now, I've been letting Nile think that we're sleeping in the house, not wanting to get his hopes up about the camper, in case it fell through somehow. But now that it's right in front of us, I tell him.

"How would you like to sleep in a camper tonight?" I ask him.

"Oh!" Nile gasps. "I would love to!"

We pull into the driveway and park by the garage, then make our way to the campers on the other side of the house. The air is filled with the smell of cut grass and the roar of the lawnmower.

"You made it!" Brice shouts.

I smile and give him a big hug. Brice is around my height, but bigger, and wears a bright red tee shirt. He's losing his hair, and so he's shaved it all off, and a bushy goatee sprouts from his chin. Combined with his countless tattoos and his sports shades, this make him look ... perhaps not entirely *scary*, but at least like he might have his own reality show centered around bounty hunting, or duck hunting, or some other type of hunting.

Brice and I have almost nothing in common. He's a supervisor at a factory in Des Moines, works at a racetrack on weekends during the summer, and serves as chief of a volunteer fire department. He'll almost certainly never move away from Iowa. But he's my oldest friend. In seventh grade, we were both on a bus to an overnight church lock-in at the YMCA (they let you swim and play basketball all night in exchange for seven dollars and the opportunity to spend an hour telling you about Jesus), and Brice asked me if I wanted to hang out with him when we got there. Looking back, it was sort of a courageous thing for him to do. We were both unpopular already. What if I'd told him no?

We spent that night shooting pool and playing foosball together, and after that, we took turns staying over at each other's houses, renting awful movies like "Ski School" and "Porky's Revenge," hoping to catch a blurry glimpse of boobs on VHS. By high school, we'd formed a slightly larger group of friends, mostly with the girls in our class. Brice had been held back a year in school by his parents because he was such a small kindergartner, and so he was the first of us to get a driver's license. We would all pile into his rust-brown 1979 Dodge van, nicknamed "The Turd," and drive to the mall or the movie theater in Ames on weekends.

Brice introduces Nile to his kids, Maddie and Owen, and to the dog yipping at Nile's heels. Both kids are skinny and yellow-haired. Maddie is nine, and Owen is exactly Nile's age, born on the very same day as him. "Sophia!" Brice yells at the dog, and then turns to me. "Is he scared of dogs?"

Nile cowers behind me, and I put my hand on top of his head. "Oh, yeah."

"She won't bite," Brice assures us.

Owen, who is a head shorter than Nile and seems to have his mouth permanently affixed in a mischievous grin, leads Nile to our camper and begins giving us a tour. Brice has brought his own, smaller pop-up camper for his family, but this larger, luxury model belongs to his parents, and they're letting Nile and me stay in it for two nights. The air-conditioned camper has a living room with recliners and a pullout couch, a kitchen with a sink and a refrigerator, a bathroom with a shower and toilet, and a bedroom with a comfortable queen bed.

"It even has lights that you can turn on and off," Nile says, playing with a light switch. "This is even nicer than my house!"

• • •

We all make our way back into town for an event called the Pedal Pull. It's a kiddie version of a tractor pull, where children pedal special tricycle-tractors, competing to see how far they can pull a heavy, spring-loaded contraption behind them. I failed miserably at it when I was a kid, but I want Nile to give it a shot.

I pull the Black Racer up alongside Brice's car at the edge of the park, and we get out and douse the kids with sunscreen and bug spray. The kids are all excited by the sight of a giant inflatable slide decorated with characters from the Pixar "Cars" movies, but looking around, I can't help being disappointed. It's so much smaller than it used to be. There's no funnel cake stand, no games, no bingo tent. Just a half dozen smallish rides, along with some food trucks lined up on the other side of the bandstand. "Is this really it?" I say.

"Evidently," Brice answers. "I told you it wasn't much."

We walk to the big concrete slab in front of the bandstand and wait in line to register the kids for the Pedal Pull. In line, I begin seeing people I haven't seen in nearly twenty years – people who graduated with me, or a year or two before or behind me – and the encounters are more pleasant and less awkward than I would have expected. It's like a high school reunion, but without the pressure to impress. Mari, who moved back to Maxwell after a stint in the Air Force and a few years in Washington, D.C., is selling refreshments. Tank, who recently served several months in prison for DUI convictions that kept stacking on top of one another, is behind me in line, waiting to register his daughter. A girl who was a freshman when I graduated now has three kids and is hugely pregnant with a fourth. It's a little strange to see my peers running things. In my mind, they're frozen in time as kids, and I have the strange sensation that they're all merely playacting at being adults.

It takes me a moment to remember Tank's real name. Nearly everybody in Maxwell – or, at least, nearly every male – had a nickname when we were growing up, and many people were called *only* by their nicknames. Some were merely lazy plays off of people's actual names ("Cake" for Ryan Cakerice, "Full-Dog" for Brett Fuller), and some were actual names that were not the person's real name ("Fred" for Ryan, "Juan" for Andrew). But most were just completely random, with obscure origins: Tank, Flip, Booie, Pee-Wee, Moose, Bunky, Slick.

At first, Nile is excited at the sight of the miniature tractors, but as the event gets underway, he becomes nervous and skittish. A three-year-old blonde girl pedals her heart out, and the crowd cheers. "I don't want them to cheer for me so loud!" Nile says.

"You'll be fine," I tell him, trying to keep my voice light and cheerful. "After this, we'll get ice cream."

When it's time for the four- and five-year-olds to pedal, the first girl makes it 17 feet, 5 inches. The next kid, a boy, goes for 18 feet, 7 inches.

Owen's turn comes, and the crowd cheers as he pedals his little legs, pushing as hard as he can to drag the sled along the concrete. Nile covers his ears.

"21 feet, 3 inches," the woman announces into the microphone when Owen is done, and another little cheer goes up.

"All right, buddy," I say to Nile. "Your turn."

Nile just stands in front of me, looking blankly at the bright blue pedal tractor. When he makes no move to get on, I lift him onto the seat, and he grips the steering wheel, but lets his feet rest on the concrete. "I'm tired," he says.

"Okay," I tell him. "I'm going to count to three. One ... two ... three!"

Instead of pedaling, Nile closes his eyes and rests his head on the steering wheel of the little tractor. It's so cute and pathetic that I whip out my phone to take a picture. Once I have the photo, I plan to give up on the Pedal Pull and take Nile to get ice cream. I've learned my lesson from Niagara Falls. I'm not going to make him do anything he doesn't want to do.

But while I'm snapping pictures, Nile very slowly starts to pedal. He keeps his forehead on the steering wheel the whole time, never opening his eyes, and he just barely succeeds at inching the tractor forward. The crowd roars as though he's doing great.

Finally, Nile stalls out. "14 feet, 4 inches," the woman announces.

"Come here, buddy." I lift him off the tractor and wrap him into a hug.

Nile sobs a couple of times – big, surprising sobs – and for a moment I worry that I've ruined everything again. But in another instant, he's over it. "Daddy," he says, looking up at me, clutching his participation ribbon. "I tried my very best."

• • •

We let the kids go on a couple of rides at the park, and then head to the town museum on Main Street, where Brice's wife Christina meets us. The museum's displays are impressive, if a bit random. There are rooms made up to look like old school houses and general stores, but there are also old Peruvian coins, a copy of a French newspaper from the day after FDR died, and a jar labeled "$1,000 or More of Shredded Money." There are extensive collections of pencils, geodes, seashells, license plates, and barbed wire. The basement is full of ancient farm equipment. On a table on the first floor, a tattered orange swim cap sits on a white Styrofoam dummy head, on which someone has scrawled in black Sharpie, "Remember when we all wore bathing caps?"

We come to a hallway with all the Maxwell High senior portraits, from before the schools combined with Collins, and I find my grandfather in the class of 1949. Papa stares out at me from behind the glass, eighteen years old, his hair neatly parted, beaming and dressed in a striped suit jacket. In his grin, I see my own big front teeth. I see the squinty eyes that Nile and I share. Unlike in the photos in Alice's basement, Papa looks happy and hopeful, filled with energy. His entire life is in front of him.

In another room, I'm surprised to find a photograph of myself. It's part of an exhibit called "Citizens of Tomorrow," featuring the donated school portraits of a bunch of kids from the 1990s, their preteen awkwardness enshrined forever. Alice must have sent them my picture. It's quite something. I'm twelve years old in the shot, wearing a sweater vest over a denim shirt and holding Alice's pet Shih Tzu Bridgett, smiling like an idiot.

Brice cracks up when he sees the picture, then leans down and snaps a photo of the photograph with his cell phone, so he can show our other friends and make fun of me later on. "I'm glad I'm not in any of these," he says, putting his phone away.

We leave the room and follow the kids to a display on military uniforms. "Whatever," I say. "I'm immortal now."

. . .

After the museum, Nile and I slip away, telling Brice we'll meet up again later. I stop at Casey's to get Nile a strawberry frosted donut, and then we drive toward the cemetery. I don't know when we'll get another chance to go, and something about seeing Papa's picture in the museum makes this feel like the right time.

"You watched 'Charlotte's Web' three times with Grandma Alice," I say to Nile during the short drive. "What happens to Charlotte at the end?"

"Um, um, um," Nile says. "She dies."

"She dies," I repeat. "How did that make you feel?"

"Sad."

"Remember how we've talked about how everything that lives, dies someday?" I point out the window. "Like those flowers. Those flowers will die." Nile is silent, and I press on. "And Grandma Alice's dog. It'll die one day, too."

"Oh," Nile says. "I did not know that dogs die."

"They're alive," I say. "So they die."

"Yeah," Nile says. The word comes out of his mouth like a sigh. "I will die, too, but not right now. I'm too small to die."

We drive past my old house, to the very edge of town, and park alongside the cemetery. It's an unfenced, spawning swath of land, bright green and neatly manicured, with clusters of tombstones bookending a large patch of virgin grass in the middle.

We get out of the car, and I hand Nile his donut. "Here we are," I tell him. "This is where my grandfather is buried."

"Oh," Nile says, taking a bite from the donut. "Is he a fossil?"

"No, baby. It takes a long time for dead things to become fossils."

I scan the headstones, seeing the family names of old neighbors and classmates: Golly, McCord, Stigler, Horn, Robertson, Law. "You see these stones, Nile? That means someone dead is buried under there."

"Right there?" he asks, pointing to a low, rectangular monument.

"Right there," I say. "And there, and there, and there."

Then I spot it. A distinctive triangular stone with "HENNICK" engraved right in the middle. A few bouquets of fake red and blue flowers sprout up from the base, and when we come closer, I can see Papa's name carved into the left side of the stone, his brother's name into the right. Papa's parents, who both died before I was born, are buried right next to them. I used to come visit this spot when I was a boy, to see my last name carved on a stone above the dead bodies of relatives I never met.

I pull Nile close to me and stand looking at the grave marker. "Do you want to hear some happy memories about my grandpa?"

Nile takes another bite from his donut. "Yes."

"When I was a little boy, we went to the toy store every Saturday," I tell him. "We called it 'Special Day,' and I could pick out any toy I wanted, as long as it came in a small box. And then we would go back to his house, and he would make me snacks, and I would sit on his lap and watch TV with him."

"Oh, that's nice," Nile says, indulging me. "Did he tickle you?"

"His whiskers tickled me, when I rubbed against his cheek."

"People don't have whiskers," Nile says. "Not like a cat!"

"Not like a cat, baby."

"What else did your grandfather do when he was alive?"

"He worked at a bank, and then he retired," I say. "That means when people get older and they stop working. And then he moved here to Maxwell for a while, and after that he moved to a place called Las Vegas. It has lots of flashing lights, just like Niagara Falls, and lots of hotels with swimming pools. You'd like it there."

Papa died six months after he left me that voicemail on Christmas Eve, six months after I stopped speaking to him. He'd been hospitalized in Las Vegas for one of the health problems that had been plaguing him, and he never made it out of the ICU. When I heard the news, I felt numb. There wasn't any funeral, and I wouldn't have traveled back for it anyway, but I wanted to do something to mourn him. I thought about buying a bunch of baseball cards and organizing them by team, but I didn't know what I'd do with them afterward. I thought about playing blackjack, but the nearest casino was more than two hours away. Instead, I drove to a horse track thirty miles south of Boston. There wasn't any live racing, but it was the day of the Belmont Stakes, and the place was packed with people betting on the simulcast. I stayed for a couple of hours, wagering conservatively and leaving slightly ahead, which wasn't a fitting tribute at all.

That night, after we put Nile to bed, there was a message on my phone from Papa's number. I listened to it and heard the voice of his girlfriend. "I want you to know," Marie said, her voice breaking with grief, "that he loved you very, very, very much. I just needed you to know that. Even after the letter. But as stubborn as he was, he wasn't about to call you first. And I'm so sorry you felt that way."

I called her back. I told her that I loved Papa and knew he loved me, and Marie said that Papa knew, too.

But here's the thing. I don't regret not talking to him those last six months. I don't regret that I never said goodbye.

We had our time. It ended.

At the graveside, I pull Nile close to me again. I'm crying a little, and I want to let the moment stretch out, want to feel whatever feelings I have about this, and then to be done with it. But I know that's not how this works. Fathers never truly stay buried. Ghosts never give up their right to haunt you.

"Come here, baby," I say to Nile. "Stand here and eat your donut and give me a nice hug."

Nile does give me a hug, but then he gets restless, and soon he wanders off to look at the other monuments. "Daddy?" he says, pointing at a stone. "Daddy, who's buried right here?"

"Give me a minute, buddy."

"Look," Nile says. "There's a fire chief sign in front of this stone. I guess a firefighter got buried here. What's his name?

I keep my eyes on the gravestone markings for Papa and his father, studying the dates. His dad was born in 1911, exactly a hundred years before Nile. I think of my father, my grandfather, and my great-grandfather, and then I look up at Nile, poking around amongst the graves, and I think about how he wouldn't be here if it weren't for these men.

"Daddy!" he shouts. "Come on! Who's this firefighter who's buried here? Tell me."

"Coming!" I call back. But first, I take a folded sheet of paper from my pocket. It's the letter I wrote last night in Alice's basement. I tuck the paper into the fake flowers and then stand up and take one last look at the stone. "Goodbye, Papa."

Still sniffling, I join Nile, who wants me to read every gravestone to him. I thought he would be scared of the cemetery, but he's bouncing around, looking for the little markers that signify a dead firefighter or police officer or war veteran. We make our way back to the Black Racer, and I buckle Nile in, ready to leave this death and sadness behind us and join our friends.

As we pull away, I think about my letter. When I sat down to write it, I meant for it to be a positive thing, an attempt to do what Jane talked about: accepting Papa for who he was, rather than resenting him for who he wasn't. "You can't disappoint me anymore," I wrote at the beginning. "So I'll write down the things I wish you'd done, things I know you'll never do now, and then I'll try to let them go."

But as I listed the things I wished he'd done – raised my father better, stood up to Alice, stayed with me after he adopted me, kept in touch after he left – I found myself getting angry with him all over again. "Christ," I wrote. "I hoped this would be cathartic. I hoped I would get to the end of this letter and thank you for all the things you did for me when I was a little boy. By now, I thought I'd be reminiscing about the good times. But it turns out that being a shitty father might be the one thing I can't forgive. And you were a shitty father. Now you'll never have a chance to make things right."

"If you're anything but ashes now, I hope you've found peace," I wrote at the end. "I have work to do here. I have a son to raise."

· · ·

We meet Brice and his family for dinner back at the park, where things have finally picked up. It's still not the same Old Settlers I remember from years ago, but it's no longer completely dead. Kids shriek on the rides, and farmers eat with their families under the big tent near the bandstand, waiting for the rodeo to start. I get Nile a slice of pizza from a food truck, and order myself a "walking taco," which is a bag of Doritos with seasoned beef, cheese, lettuce, tomato, and sour cream all stuffed inside, served with a fork and napkin.

We eat at a picnic table, and a parade of old friends and acquaintances streams by. Some are surprised to see me, but others let out only the barest chuckle of recognition and then greet me with a casual, "Hey, Calvin," as though we just saw each other last Tuesday. I don't fool myself into thinking that I could live here again, but I also don't feel out of place. Not since college have I run into so many people I know in one spot. I forget entirely that there's anything different about Nile, up until I see a black teenage boy walk by with a group of his white friends, and I find myself wondering the same thing other people must think when they see my son: *What's he doing here?*

We finish our food and walk over to the trailers lining the rodeo arena, browsing amongst spurs, bandanas, cowboy boots, and neon lassoes. "Amie" plays over the arena's speakers while we poke around. One table is full of tee shirts with slogans like "The Second Amendment is My Gun Permit" and "I'm All for Gun Control, I Use Both Hands." Just the sheer aggression of the slogans sets me on my heels a bit, never mind the fact that the people who buy them will presumably be well-armed.

Owen picks out a black cowboy hat with blue blinking lights at the six points of a silver sheriff's star, and he looks hilarious wearing it with his neon green Batman tee shirt, jean shorts, and tall cowboy boots. I offer to buy Nile a hat, but he says he doesn't want one.

"You don't want a cowboy hat?" I say. "I really have made you into a city boy."

"I just don't want one!" he says. "Okay? OKAY?!?!"

I let the outburst slide without comment. He's tired.

We all head inside the arena, where we run into Brett and Courtney, who graduated with Brice and me, and who were named homecoming king and queen during our senior year of high school. They have a boy named Nolan who's a year older than Nile and Owen, and a daughter the same age as Peanut, and we all find seats together in the top couple rows of the bleachers.

It's not yet dusk, but the shadows elongate as the sun prepares to set, stretching out over the middle of the muddy rodeo oval. As the crowd settles in, I spot a handful of cowboy hats, but more people are wearing Hawkeyes or Cyclones or John Deere gear. At seven o'clock, the emcee, a stocky man in a green button-down and a white cowboy hat, rides out into the middle of the oval on a white horse, holding a wireless microphone in one hand. "Ladies and gentlemen," he says, his voice echoing over the PA. "Who's proud of this great nation that we live in?"

A big whoop goes up from the crowd.

"Tonight is a celebration of American heritage and the cowboy's way of life," the emcee says. "If you haven't already, I ask you to stand with me, and please remove your hats."

I expect the national anthem to begin playing, but instead, after a brief pause, the man leads the crowd in prayer. "Our most gracious and heavenly father, tonight we ..." he begins.

"The horse!" Nile says.

I shush him quietly.

"But I was whispering."

"... the many blessings you bestow upon us each and every moment," the emcee continues. "As cowboys and cowgirls, we don't ask for any special favors. We only ask that you help us to compete as honest as the horses we ride, and in a manner as clean and pure as the wind that blows across this great land of ours. So when we do make that last ride that is inevitable for us all to make, to that place up there where the grass grows green and lush and stirrup high, you'll tell us, 'Come on in, cowboy. Your entry fees have been paid in full.' Amen."

Then, the national anthem starts, a recording playing over the loudspeakers. Maddie, Owen, and Nolan all dutifully place their right hands over their hearts, but Nile has never been to any sort of organized sporting event, and he doesn't know what he's supposed to do.

"Like this," I whisper, patting my chest to show him where to put his hand. But he misunderstands me and pats his own chest, thumping away with his palm until the end of the song.

The first event is saddle bronc riding. There's great fanfare leading up to the opening of the chute. The emcee hypes up the first rider, backgrounded by a heavy metal guitar riff. But then, the chute opens, and the rider lasts not quite two seconds before he's bucked over the head of his horse. The cowboy goes sailing through the air, and I think he'll end up with a face full of mud, but he catches himself with his hands just as he hits the ground.

Brice and Brett and I trade old stories, and Nile forms his own little-boy tribe with Owen and Nolan, stomping on the bleachers and shouting nonsense about dinosaurs and fire trucks. Occasionally, we tell them to pipe down, but we mostly leave them to themselves. This has started happening more and more the past few months, when there are both adults and little kids around. Nile and I retreat to our own separate camps and almost forget about each other for a while. It's so different from when he was three and four years old, when he needed me every second.

"My jetpack!" Owen shouts.

Nile giggles and jumps up and down on the bleachers. "Aggggh! I'm floating off into space. Help!"

"Oh, no!" Nolan says. "Get in the moon buggy!"

Instantly, their bodies all shake from the bumps of the imaginary moon buggy ride. Somehow, they all know the rules of this game that they're making up as they go along.

Brice explains the rodeo events to me as they come up. Calf roping starts, and he tells me all the different ways the cowboys can lose points. The first contestant rides out on his horse, twirling his lasso above his head, and then snares a little black calf around the neck. The calf tries to run off, but the noose tightens and he falls to the ground, lying immobile and choking in the mud. The cowboy jumps off his horse and runs over to the calf, picks the animal up, and throws it back down to the ground again before tying up its legs.

"Yeah," I say. "How is this not torture?"

"It's either this," Brice says, "or end up a cheeseburger."

Nile taps me on the shoulder. "Daddy?" he says. "When are they going to be done with this cow part?"

"You don't like it?" I ask him.

Nile shakes his head. "Cows don't like the mud," he says. "Only pigs."

"It'll be done soon," I tell him.

Nile's and my shared squeamishness makes me think of the original purpose of this trip – the purpose, really, of coming to this rodeo, of sitting in these seats, of watching this cowboy body-slam this calf: to contemplate what it means to be a man, and what it means to raise one. I can feel our time running out, and my mind races through the little lessons I've tried to give Nile in the Black Racer on the way out here, about how a good man takes care of his family and respects women, how a good man is kind, how he works hard. It all feels so quaint, so obvious, so generic. So divorced from any of the specific context that will determine what exactly the world will expect from my son.

I think about how different things would be for him if he were growing up in Maxwell instead of suburban Boston, if his friends and classmates wore cutoff tee shirts and worked on cars and wiped grease on their jeans. I look around the crowd and do what Belzie calls a "black count," hunting for visual evidence of people of color. I find only the black teenager I saw earlier, sitting across the arena with his friends. I wonder what his life is like, what it means to be a brown boy in Maxwell at this precise moment in time. There was a half-black boy on one of the track teams we ran against, and in junior high, the boys on our team all called him "Grayboy." I wonder if this kid at the rodeo has to deal with this shit still. If he does, I'm sure some people tell him, "Be a man, stand up for yourself." And I'm sure other people tell him, "Be a man, walk away."

The sky turns black and the lights come up as the rest of the events go by – steer wrestling, barrel racing – until finally it's time for the main event: bull riding. A rock version of "Smooth Criminal" plays over the PA as the crowd waits for the first rider, and then the gate opens. The bull comes storming out, and the cowboy is already halfway off the animal's back from the very beginning. He bounces straight up into the air once, lands back on the bull, and then loses his balance and falls forward onto the beast's neck. He rides like that, in horizontal limbo, for just another fraction of a second, and then the bull bucks again, and the cowboy tumbles off in a violent barrel roll.

The bull's hind legs nearly catch the cowboy's head on the way down, but then the rodeo clown distracts the animal and leads it toward an opening in the pen. Only when the rider pushes himself up out of the muck and runs out of the arena do I realize why he looks odd to me. He's not wearing a cowboy hat. In its place, he has on a black helmet with a face mask. He looks more like a hockey goalie than a cowboy. I smirk to myself. Every time some school bans dodgeball, or some new safety measure gets put in place to prevent brain damage in football players, a chorus of macho men materializes to denounce the "pussification of America." If even cowboys are wearing protective headgear, maybe the macho men are losing.

I've only been half paying attention during most of the rodeo, but now I'm rapt, waiting to see one of the cowboys pull off a glorious ride that lasts beyond the eight-second buzzer. But the second rider fares even worse than the first, getting bucked almost before the gate opens. "Put your hands together," the emcee implores the crowd as cowboy jogs off, dejected. "That's not the ride he hoped for, but let's give him some consolation enthusiasm."

It goes on like this down the line. One rider stays on for two seconds, the next for three, the next for two. No one gets close to eight. And then, before I know it, the rodeo is over, and we file out with the rest of the crowd.

For all the buildup, this rodeo was just a rodeo. I came here seeking grand answers about what it means to be a man and a father, and instead I got to eat a walking taco and witness a handful of blink-and-you'll-miss-them bull rides. It's impossible to know ahead of time which moments will be significant, which will have something to teach us. Nine months from today, just before he turns six years old, I will take Nile to his first Red Sox game at Fenway, along with Belzie's father. It will be the day after Boston fans are in the news for throwing peanuts and hurling racial slurs at Baltimore Orioles outfielder Adam Jones, and we'll arrive early, taking our seats high in the grandstand along the first-base line. A young Kenyan woman will perform the national anthem, and I'll show Nile all over again how to put his hand over his heart, and when the song is over, the singer will receive a nice ovation from the crowd.

And then, the fan next to me, a white man in his early fifties, will lean over to me and complain, "It was too long, and she niggered it up!"

"Excuse me?" I'll say, thinking I've misheard him somehow.

"I said, 'It was too long, and she niggered it up.'"

"Just to be clear," I'll ask, still incredulous, repeating the hateful word in order to make absolutely sure I've heard what I thought I've heard. "You're saying the singer 'niggered up' the national anthem?"

"That's right," the man will say with pride. "And I stand by it."

At first, I will be confused about why the man would say this on this night of all nights, right after the Jones incident, and why he would say it to me of all people, sitting with my black family. *Didn't he see my son?* I'll wonder. *Didn't he see my father-in-law?* And then I will think, *Of course he saw them, that's the whole point – finding a way to call a little boy a "nigger" and get away with it.*

I will go and find an usher and tell him what happened, and he will notify security, and I will be asked to identify the man. The man will deny, to my face, saying what he'd been so proud to say only ten minutes earlier. By the end of the night, Sox representatives will later tell me, the man will be kicked out, and will finally confess to what he said. And by the end of the next day, he will be banned from Fenway for life.

On that night at the ballpark, I won't tell Nile what happened. He'll watch Chris Sale strike out eleven batters and cheer as Hanley Ramirez hits two solo shots out of the park. He'll eat ice cream. He'll have a great time.

But then, the story will be picked up in the press, and so,

to prepare him in case anyone brings it up at school, I will sit with Nile in the kitchen on the morning of his sixth birthday, and I will try to explain the situation in terms he can understand. "The man sitting next to us said a bad word about black people," I'll tell him, "and now he can't come back to the ballpark anymore."

At first, Nile will very sweetly suggest that the man be allowed to come back if he apologizes. But then, very quickly, he'll process the news in several different ways. He'll defend the Kenyan woman's singing, saying, "She sang nice!" He'll worry what will happen if the man comes to our house, or if he shows up again at the ballpark wearing a disguise. He'll list every dark-skinned member of his family and insist, "I can still be with them! Even though they have brown skin, I can still be with them!"

Most heartbreakingly, Nile will say, "Daddy, I thought it was over, black people and white people not getting along."

And I will cry a little, and I will have to tell him that no, it's not over, it's never over.

It will be a moment when Nile loses a bit of his innocence, when he realizes that the story of race and racism in America is more complicated than the *we-used-to-do-bad-things-but-then-we-stopped* version I told him about Jackie Robinson and segregation before we visited the Hall of Fame. After this, I expect, these lessons will come more and more quickly, until his innocence is erased, until he understands the reality of things far better than I do.

• • •

After the rodeo, Brice and I drive the kids to his sister's house, one of the big ones in the subdivision at the edge of town. His nieces have agreed to watch them while we go to the country western dance back at the park. When I was a teenager, the dance was a chance for me to feel grown-up, to stay out late and slow dance with girls I was too shy to ask out on a date. But now, Brett and Brice and I camp out at a picnic table with a few classmates and resume telling old stories. I buy a round of beers for everybody, but stick to Diet Pepsi myself.

Brice has a package of chewing tobacco, and in the spirit of experimentation, I take a dip, stuffing the wet, loose chew into my lower lip. It's terrible, like a piece of gum made out of cigarettes. I spit it out after a couple of minutes.

"God," I say. "Does anybody have a toothbrush?"

Brice gives me a look. "Man up."

"How come everything that's supposed to be 'manly' is actually just stupid?" I say.

We stay out until 2 a.m., getting biscuits and gravy and coffee at the church-run food stand before heading out to pick up the children. When we arrive at the house, the kids are all sprawled out on the floor in the dark, and I pick Nile up carefully, trying not to wake him. I get his body up in front of my chest, and instinctively, he wraps his legs around me and rests his warm, heavy head on my shoulder. When I step out of the house with him, he whimpers a little from the surprise of the cool night air. "Shhh," I say, kissing his head. "It's okay. You're fine. Everything is fine."

Before I open the car door to buckle him in, I look up at the sky for a moment. It's filled with stars, and it looks so much bigger, somehow, than the night sky in Boston. For a moment, I can feel the infinity of it.

Nile, still asleep, shifts his head on my shoulder, and a little moan escapes from some unconscious place inside him. "It's okay," I say. "Daddy's here. Daddy will always be here."

Day 10

THE DAWN LIGHT WAKES ME in the camper, but Nile remains fast asleep, and I pick up the shoebox of photographs I found at Alice's house and look through them while I wait for him to get up. On top are pictures I took with disposable cameras in high school—blurry, too close snapshots of friends and girlfriends, the faces all washed out in the flash. But underneath are dozens of pictures from when my brothers and I were little. I see my six-year-old self, dressed in a ragged Santa costume that I apparently made myself, complete with a white paper beard Scotch-taped to my face. I see my four-year-old self petting a goat at a zoo. I see my brothers and me in front of the Christmas tree, each of us holding a present and grinning from ear to ear.

There are a few pictures of my dad. My mom long ago threw away most of her photos of him, and aside from the ones on his Flickr account, these are the first I've seen in a long time. I flip through them, looking for some evidence of what our life together was like, but the pictures are inscrutable. In one photo, my brothers and I are goofing around while my mom tries to corral us, and my dad stares straight into the camera, half a smile on his face. In another, he's sitting at the dinner table with Papa, my mom, and me. My mom is looking over her shoulder, flashing a smile at the camera, and Papa has a goofy look on his face, like he's been interrupted mid-bite. But my dad is slightly in the shadows, looking askance at the photographer with his mouth closed. One is a family portrait taken when I was a newborn. I'm fat-cheeked and big-headed, gazing up at the ceiling, and my mom is smiling and pretty and impossibly young. But my dad, sitting behind her with the collar of his dress shirt poking out from beneath a white sweater, is totally expressionless.

Looking at the pictures reminds me that this whole trip – the hotels, the rides, the games, the camper, even the Black Racer – will fade for Nile, little by little, until the memories are erased completely. All he'll be left with is the photographs. The pictures will be nice to have, but they're not the same as memories, which are what we rely on to tell ourselves the stories of our lives. They're how we make meaning out of all the chaos. But the memories fade, until all that's left, often, is a single dominant feeling, a few words to stand in for entire experiences. I look at Nile, his damp head resting heavily on the pillow, and I think about the decades stretching out in front of him. I think about how, one day, everything that I am now will be reduced to a single thought, a single feeling, a single story that he tells himself about the man his father was.

When I've looked through all the photos, I type my dad's email address into the email search bar on my phone. I'm looking for the email he sent me during my senior year of college, the one that finally caused me to stop talking to him for good. But it's buried beneath emails he sent me afterward, messages I've never responded to, messages I forgot about. I remembered him sending me emails on and off for a few years, but I didn't remember there being this many. I count them up. Forty-one. Forty-one times, my father has contacted me, and forty-one times, I've ignored him.

I start reading through the messages, and I remember why I didn't respond to them. In the emails, my father wasn't apologizing. He didn't ask me to give him another chance. Instead, he sent me death notices for distant relatives I barely remembered.

He sent me a link to something called the Great Iowa Treasure Hunt, which showed that the state owed my mom thirty-five dollars in unclaimed funds. He sent me an animated video of a cat wearing headphones and dancing to hip-hop.

Only a few of the emails were more personal. In the very first, sent nearly a year after the *you'll-die-from-a-spike-in-the-chest* email, my father wrote that he was about to get on a plane to New York to visit a woman he'd met online, and told me to call him if I felt like it. In another, he attached scans of letters I wrote to him when I was in the third grade, after my mom had moved us to Massachusetts but before he followed us out there, in which I thanked him for sending us baseballs and promised to send him one of the little stories I liked to write. One of the last emails, sent seven years ago, is just a memory my father had of me dancing to Michael Jackson's "Billy Jean" at a pizza parlor when I was two years old. "While you were standing in front of the juke box, this song came on, and you proceeded to show us some dance steps we had never seen you do," he wrote. "It was a beautiful moment to remember, but we had a hard time containing ourselves, except when you looked our way."

I read this email, and my heart threatens to open up a little bit. In these couple of sentences, I see a glimmer of how I feel for my own son. But then I think, what if this were the best I could do for Nile? What if I were to disappear for the next thirty years, getting drunk in my mother's basement, only popping up occasionally to make him feel bad about himself? And then my heart snaps back shut.

• • •

Nile and I head into town early for the parade. The grass is still dewy as we walk from the camper to the Black Racer. It's a beautiful, blue-sky morning, and the sun reflects off of the pewter-colored sheet clouds that sit in the sky like glaciers. I buckle Nile into his carseat and then get into the driver's seat and pull out of the long driveway and onto the gravel leading toward the highway.

"Did you have fun with Owen and Maddie last night?" I ask Nile.

He lets out a little grunt. "Yes, I had fun." His voice is almost angry as he says this, and then it turns sad. "But I'm just going to miss them when we leave."

"We'll see them another time," I tell him. "You can't get sad every time something fun ends."

"And what about Grandma Wilson's house?" Nile says. "We need to come back, because I never even saw it!"

"We'll try to go sometime."

"But how will we get past your father?"

"Um. Maybe we can go while he's at the store."

"What if he comes back and sees you? And what if Mommy was there? If Mommy was there, we would have to hide her."

"Why would we have to hide Mommy?"

"Because!" Nile says. "She has brown skin. Your daddy doesn't like people with brown skin, and Mommy has brown skin!"

"Okay, baby," I say, trying to settle him down. "That's not the reason we didn't go to see my daddy, anyway."

"We didn't go see him because he's rude," Nile says. "After you told him that he wasn't a good daddy, he said, 'I don't want to be your daddy anymore.' Remember?"

Nile is repeating almost the exact words I used to explain this to him after we left Waterloo. I'm surprised by how much he's picked up, how much he remembers. How closely he's been listening.

"I remember, baby."

"Why didn't the police just arrest him?"

"The police can't arrest you for that," I tell Nile. "It's not illegal to be a bad father."

"Why did your daddy say that?" Nile asks. "When you told him he wasn't a very good daddy, why didn't he say, 'Okay, I'll change my attitude'? Why didn't he say that?"

Throughout the trip, I've struggled with the question of how much I should tell Nile, and for the most part, I've erred on the side of telling him everything. Nile is strangely easy to talk to. Although I have to sanitize my stories and find a way to tell them so that they make sense to a five-year-old, this almost makes things easier, because it gives me permission to use the sort of simple, unsophisticated language where the truth so often resides. I've never before considered Nile's question – *Why didn't my dad try to make things right?* – but now that he's asked it in such stark terms, the answer seems obvious.

"I think he didn't say that," I tell Nile, "because I don't think he loves me."

We hit the edge of town, and I glance at the clock. The parade won't start for another hour. It's time to do what I've been putting off. It's time to "deal with" my father.

I'm not sure what this is supposed to look like. I'm not even sure what it means. I already left my father behind in Waterloo, and there's not even a special place where I can go and think about the good times, the way I did at Papa's grave. My father is still alive. And there weren't really any good times.

With nowhere else to go, I drive us to the park. There are just a few carnival workers getting things ready for the day, and I pull up alongside the baseball field and get Nile out of the car. His backpack, containing his ball from the

Cooperstown souvenir shop, is at his feet, and I pick it up, thinking I can toss him some grounders. I've very conscious that I'm constructing a moment here. It feels contrived, artificial, like nothing that comes from this could possibly be meaningful. I think about last night's rodeo, how I built it up in my mind for well over a thousand miles, and it ended up being just some guys falling off some horses. But I promised myself that I would try.

"Nile," I say. "Go stand by second base. The middle one."

He ambles over to the middle of the infield, and I stay by third base. I unzipper Nile's little backpack and pull out the baseball, then roll it to him over the dirt. But instead of throwing himself on the ball like he did at the Hall of Fame, Nile just watches it dribble past him.

"I don't want to play baseball," he says. "I want to play with my volcano truck."

"Your what?"

"My volcano truck. I want to play with my Lego volcano truck."

"It's back at the camper."

"No, it's not," Nile says, walking toward me, leaving the ball behind. "It's right here." He grabs the backpack and reaches to the bottom and pulls out the truck.

"That's fine," I tell him. "Go and play."

Nile takes the little truck over to one of the dugouts and pushes it back and forth on the metal bench. I retrieve the baseball, then walk with it to the pitcher's mound. The distance to home plate seems so much shorter than it did when I was a kid. I wish I had someone to catch for me, to see whether I'm finally able to throw a strike. Instead, I just toss the ball in the air and catch it in my bare hand.

Belzie texted me after we left Waterloo, asking if I'd gone to see my dad. When I told her I hadn't, she asked why. "Too many reasons to list," I wrote back. For one, I didn't want to bring Nile around him. My dad is a cancer and a toxin, and if I can help it, I don't expose my children to cancers and toxins. Second, I gave up long ago on the idea that my father could ever be what I need him to be. Third, even if he were capable of changing, it's too late. I don't need a father anymore. I needed a father thirty years ago, and he wasn't there. Fourth, he's never showed any real interest in reconciliation, not even in those forty-one emails he sent after I quit speaking with him. Fifth, I'm afraid that being around him will turn me back into a meek little boy again. And sixth, I'm stubborn.

Standing here now, I wonder if the real reason is what I told Nile earlier, that my father never loved me, that there was never anything there worth salvaging in the first place. But as soon as I think this, it's replaced by another thought: That I've *done* this already, that I confronted my father all those years ago, and his answer was, "You're not my son, and I hope you get murdered in New York."

I've had near strangers tell me I should talk to my father again, often without knowing any of the details of our relationship. It's not me that these people are worried about. It's their own need for a redemptive story arc, their need to believe that everything can be solved with some bullshit, third-act, father-son game of catch.

In her texts, Belzie said I should at least email my father, should at least try to get some information from him. I should ask him to elaborate on my mom's "blue baby" story of my birth, she said, should try to get him to tell me his version of my childhood. But I don't care about any of that. The bare facts don't mean anything to me at this point.

If I had to boil everything down, here is what I would want my father to tell me: *What is the matter with you? Why are you like this? How could you possibly be who you are?*

And if I got answers to these questions, then maybe I could finally answer something even more important: *What is the matter with me?*

If I thought I'd get an answer to that, I might reach out to my father. But I know I wouldn't.

And yet, here I am. To *deal* with things. Whatever that means.

"Yeah!" Nile shouts, playing with his truck. "Now let's go get that crook. Where did he go?"

Part of me feels like previous generations had it figured out. If you had a shitty father, so what? You ignored it, persevered, survived, moved on. That's what I've been trying to do. I've made my father into a person who doesn't exist, and a person who doesn't exist is a person who can't hurt me.

But that's not really true. I experience my father as an absence – as the fact of something missing – but that absence is a like black hole, exerting its own unseen gravitational force on me, always lurking, waiting to suck me in and rip me apart. The drinking, the depression, the anxiety, the constant need for love and affection. The paralyzing obsession with being the best father I can be. The near-certainty that I'm failing. It's all got to be connected. I may go weeks without thinking about my father, but he's present in a million little things I do every day.

I know I'm supposed to be angry with my father, and so I try to feel it. But there's nothing. Just numbness. Maybe I'm not fooling myself, I think. Maybe this is healthy, appropriate. I can't walk around all the time with a knife sticking out of my heart. At a certain point, I have to live my life.

When I've tried to play out the scene of seeing my dad again in my mind, it's never been anything close to satisfying. I would show up, and there would be an awkward hello. A ridiculous handshake, maybe. Definitely no hug. My dad would clear his throat a lot, and if Nile were there, he would say something disarmingly honest like, "My daddy says you don't like brown people," and my father would chuckle as though any of this were funny. And then my Grandma Wilson would do most of the talking, asking after Belzie and Peanut, and at some point my father would disappear to the backyard to fiddle with his hummingbird feeders.

Even the fantasy is too lame to get worked up about.

I think to what Belzie said, about how I should ask my father about some basic facts, and even though I don't care about that stuff, and even though my father *isn't even here*, I give it a shot.

"Tell me about when I was born," I imagine myself saying.

"I was so proud to be a father," my father responds in my mind. "I looked at you in the little hospital bassinet, and I knew – "

Fuck you.

The anger is visceral. Immediate. Surprising. In the abstract, I'm numb. But as soon as I give my father a voice, the feelings boil over in an instant.

I know I'm not being fair. It's not my father's fault that I've imagined him bullshitting me with the loving father routine, and so I give him another shot.

"Tell me about when I was born," I say again.

"I knew I wasn't ready for it," I imagine my father saying. "You weren't planned, and I was young, and we didn't have much money – "

Double fuck you.

"What led to you and Mom splitting up?" I ask him.

"You know how she can be," my father says. "All the constant nagging – "

Fuck you forever.

"Try again," I say. "Why did you and Mom split up?"

"It was my fault," this version of my father says. "I never grew up, and I was drinking and drugging still, and – "

Fuck you fuck you fuck you fuck you.

I won't let him get a sentence out, not even in my mind. Every single response I can fathom sends me into a fist-clenched rage. I look over at Nile, still playing with his truck, and I wonder what sort of answer I could possibly give him if I disappeared for decades.

There is no such an answer. There would be nothing to say.

"Why are you like this?" I ask my dad.

In my mind, he responds, "Because I could never be any other way."

Maybe it's true. But I don't care.

Fuck you.

I'm still holding Nile's baseball, and I cock my arm, readying to throw it into the backstop. But then I stop myself. I bring the ball back down in front of my face, and I look at it and squeeze it, and instead of trying to release my anger, I try to feel it as fully as I can. *Fuck you.* It's a mantra. *Fuck you.* The words feel pure and simple and true. *Fuck you fuck you fuck you.*

I always hear about people "letting go" of their anger. But to me, that feels like a fairy tale. The *fuck you* will always be there for me, will always be ready to pop up to the surface if my father gets too close. The *fuck you* isn't some sort of childish grudge-holding. The *fuck you* is me being an adult about things. It's me acknowledging that not everything has a happy ending, that my father isn't going to suddenly show up and make things right.

And the *fuck you* is something else, too. It's me saying that I'll never forgive my father and my grandfather for being who they were. And this is why: Because if I forgive them, I give myself permission to become them.

This whole trip, I've been trying to answer the question, "What sort of man am I going to be?" For all the complexity about class and race and gender roles and societal expectations, it now occurs to me that there are really only two possible answers: I can be a man like my father, or I can be a different sort of man. All this time, that's what I've been afraid of. Turning into my dad. And in this moment, I know that I won't. My anger won't let me.

I watch Nile playing, and I know it in my bones. I'm never going to leave. If the rest of the world comes toppling down around me, if I start drinking and can't stop, if Belzic and I divorce … it doesn't matter. Nile will always know that his daddy is there for him, no matter what.

The *fuck you* is my line in the sand. It's me saying that I cannot do this shit to my own children, because if I do, I've already said that there's no coming back from it. I don't get to float back into their lives one day for some bullshit Precious Moments reunion. The *fuck you* is my way of burning my lifeboats, my way of ensuring that I only get this one chance.

I have to be honest with myself, though. Even if Nile weren't a consideration, I'm almost certain I'd never speak to my father again. I have many good reasons, reasons I've gone over time and again in my head. But part of it is pure spite.

Lots of fathers abandon their sons. Not many sons get the chance to abandon their fathers back. I'm not giving that up.

• • •

When we arrive at the parade, both sides of Main Street are packed with people. The adults sit in lawn chairs or on the curb, and the kids stand clutching plastic bags, twitchy with anticipation of the candy that will soon be thrown their way.

We find Brice and Christina and their kids in front of the fire department.

On an average August morning in Iowa, we'd already be sweating, but it's 10:30 a.m., and a sign in front of City Hall says it's only 74 degrees. The sky is blue, and the sun is warm on my skin, but the air is dry and pleasant, not muggy. It's a perfect day for a parade.

Things kick off with a group of five military veterans carrying guns and flags. Our friend Mari is one of the marchers, balancing a purple Veterans of Foreign Wars flag out in front of her body. Next come the Boy Scouts, carrying a banner and an American flag of their own. Then a series of sporty convertibles idle down the road, each carrying elderly riders, identified by handmade signs as the parade kings and queens and grand marshals. Their middle-aged children walk alongside the cars, reaching into big bags and tossing candy toward the curbs.

Nile is timid at first, gingerly picking up a single Tootsie Roll or Dum Dum at a time and placing it into his gallon Ziploc bag. Owen is the opposite, rabidly scooping up as much candy as he can. Maddie plays mother hen, sharing her candy with Nile and showing him where to get more. As the fire trucks and floats go by, Nile becomes more comfortable. His bag starts to fill up, and at one point I have to call him back when he races off down the street to chase after a miniature Snickers bar.

A military jeep motors down the street, trailed by the high school marching band, which is bleating out a song I can't quite identify. The high school dance team comes down the street next, a troupe of bubbly girls in purple cheerleader uniforms, their bouncing ponytails tied back with white ribbons. One of them, a skinny blonde with braces, is Brice's niece, and she comes up to the kids and dumps her entire bag of lollypops in front of them.

I smile, watching the kids try to grab the candy before a second swarm of children shows up. This is our last day of the trip, and these are the sorts of memories I was hoping to create for Nile. The sun shining on his face, the blare of the fire trucks' horns, the feel of the candy in his little fist. Even if he doesn't remember the moments, I hope he'll remember the feelings.

Another hailstorm of candy sprays out from the window of a truck, sending the kids running, and I decide to play a little game. I pretend for a moment that I'm inside Nile's head, seeing the world through his eyes. It's exactly what I said I wouldn't do, trotting out E.B. White's body-swapping parlor trick. But the leap is surprisingly easy to make.

Through Nile's eyes, the world looks new to me again, fresh and unfamiliar. Everything is slightly bigger, brighter, more magical. I can feel the energy coursing through his body, his giddiness at the prospect of the next throw of candy. And I can feel his uncertainty, his nervousness, the worry that he might not be doing this right somehow, the worry that some bigger, more confident kid will come and push him out of the way. I see the man in the old-fashioned pickup truck reach down into a bag of candy and toss a handful out into the road. The candy lands at Nile's feet, and I see it, too, and his hand is my hand as he reaches down to pick it up.

Then, Nile turns and faces away from the vehicles. He searches the crowd at the curb. Still looking through his eyes, I see what I wouldn't have seen when I was a boy. I see a father watching from the curb, ready to protect him, ready to pull him back if he gets too close to the trucks, ready to tell him how many pieces of candy he's allowed to eat before lunch.

I see me.

The illusion is shattered. I'm knocked out of Nile's head, back into my own body. As I stand here watching him through my own eyes again, a thought begins to take shape in my mind. It's been a vague, nagging feeling throughout the trip, something I haven't been able to vocalize. This whole time, I haven't been trying to give Nile the father I never had. I've been trying to give *myself* the father I never had. Unconsciously, I've convinced myself that if I can just get this right, if I can just be the perfect father to Nile, then everything from the past will somehow be okay.

This is why I've been telling Nile over and over that our trip is the most fun anybody's ever had. It's why I pull him close to me and hold on for a beat too long. It's why I want all his memories to be crisp and golden and perfect. Maybe this is what dads have been doing for decades when they call out to the back seat, "Are we having fun yet? Eh? Eh?" Maybe what they're really saying is, "Am I good enough? Do I matter? Will you remember me? Will you tell everybody you meet that I was the best father in the world? Tell me you will! Tell me! Tell me before I die."

A few days ago, this realization would have made me feel selfish and childlike, the way I felt in the Chicago condo when I used Nile to make me feel better. But today, I smile. This thing that I've been chasing, it turns out, is impossible, and that takes the pressure off somehow. I can't change the past, but I can change the future.

I think back to last night, to picking Nile up and carrying his sleepy body outside and telling him, "Daddy's here." He wasn't awake to hear it. That was me telling myself what I've always needed to hear: *You're okay. You're fine. Everything is going to be okay.*

• • •

The rest of the day is a sun-drenched montage. We stop to get drinks at Logsdon's, a family-owned grocery store with three aisles and a creaky screen door, and then we all go down to the park. The kids ride the rides, and we all stuff our faces with sugar and fried foods. In the middle of the day, we go out to Brice's sister's house and swim in her large above-ground pool. Brice has an extra set of arm floats for Nile. He's tried them in the past, and has always tipped over into the water anyway, but this time he's able to hold himself upright, and I don't have to keep him within arm's reach at every moment. He and Owen splash each other and clamber over inflatable toys, and Brice and I relax in the sun.

We stay in the pool for more than an hour, and then Nile and I drive back out to Brice's parents' house in the country, where I've accidentally left some ride tickets behind. The wind has picked up, and stepping out of the Black Racer, I catch a whiff of pig shit in the air.

"Ewwww," Nile says. "Not pig poop!"

"It's fine," I tell him, smiling. "It's better than fine. It's perfect."

On the drive back into town, the road seems to stretch out forever in front of us. White clouds drift through the sky like ships, casting their shadows onto the cornfields. I have the urge to tell Nile, *Look! Remember this day! Remember when the sky was blue, and the corn was green, and you were with your daddy, and you were happy.* But I let the urge pass. Nile will remember what he remembers. Instead of trying to imprint the memory onto his little brain, I keep my focus on the landscape, and try to hold onto the moment for myself.

This isn't some magical turning point. I haven't had any grand epiphanies, and even if I had, I know myself well enough to know that I wouldn't be able to hold onto them. Life is easy today, full of sunshine and snow cones and carnival rides, but it won't stay like this forever. No matter how bright today is, there aren't any guarantees about tomorrow.

I think back to an evening last winter, one of the days when the sky turned pitch black in the early afternoon, and the wind howled outside the windows. I was depressed, and at Nile's bedtime, I pulled him close to me and told him, "I want you to be better than me when you grow up."

It was a maudlin, dramatic thing to say to a little boy, and I expected him to ignore me, to start talking about trucks or superheroes. But instead, Nile pulled his head back and looked me in the eyes. "No," he said.

"No?" I laughed lightly, shaken out of my funk. "You want to be worse than me?"

Nile put his head on my shoulder and hugged me tight, and he said, "We'll be better together, Daddy."

ACKNOWLEDGMENTS

AFTER I LEARNED THAT BILL HENDERSON and Pushcart Press would be putting out my debut memoir, someone asked me, "How does it feel to be published by a legend?" It feels amazing. Thank you, Bill, for seeing something in this book, and for your advocacy and support.

Thank you to my incredible writing group, the Chunky Monkeys. I could thank each of you limitless times for all the different ways you've helped me get here. Christopher Castellani, Chip Cheek, Jennifer De Leon, Sonya Larson, Celeste Ng, Alex Marzano-Lesnevich, Whitney Scharer, Adam Stumacher, Grace Talusan, and Becky Tuch: It is so much fun to be able to tell people that I am friends with you geniuses.

Thank you to GrubStreet, quite possibly the world's best and most supportive creative writing center. Special thanks to founder Eve Bridburg and instructors Alysia Abbott, Michelle Seaton, and Dorian Fox.

Before this book, I wrote another one. It was a novel, and it never got good, no matter how hard I worked on it – and despite the incredibly generous support of Marie Maude Evans, Matt Deos, and everyone at Sosyete Nago. Thank you so much for all your help.

Thank you to everyone who has ever tried to teach me anything, and especially to the teachers who encouraged me in my writing: Tim Bascom, Katherine Bell, Peg Evans, Julia Fierro, John Fulton, Jennifer Haigh, Sheila Severson King,

Jill McDonough, and Askold Melnyczuk.

To Kathleen McKenna, Jennifer Taber VanDerwerken, and Alexander Yates, thank you for being incisive readers, supportive friends, and generous givers of feedback. And thank you to Aaron Devine, Lisa Duffy, Jessica Moreland, and Alison Murphy for your writerly friendship. My entire writing life would have been impossible without the support of dozens of different editors, who have made me better at my craft and given me the opportunity to turn my words into my living. Special thanks to Leslie Anderson, Nancy Berry, Vanessa Bertollini, Martin Finucane, Tim Gregorski, Kelly Konrad, Matt McLaughlin, Kelly Roberson, and Michael Warshaw.

I will be forever grateful to Millicent Bennett for believing in this book, championing it, and connecting me with Pushcart Press.

Finally, thank you to my family. Mom, you're one of my best friends. Belzie, you're one of the smartest, hardest working, most sneakily funny people I know, and your belief and support has meant everything. Nile and Eloise, I've said this already in a roundabout way in the book, but I'll state again it clearly here: You two are, for me, the very meaning of life.

Calvin Hennick
2019